A STUDY OF

psalm 119

that i may live

jodi tatum

That I May Live: A Study of Psalm 119

ISBN: 978-1673644449

Printed in the United States of America

In loving memory of my grandmother

Edna Susan Springer

(1915-2002)

who delighted in the way of His Testimonies (Psalm 119:14) and
guarded her life according to His Word (Psalm 119:9).

"Your statutes have been my songs in
the house of my sojourning."

Psalm 119:54

Table of Contents

Introduction

"Give me life according to your word!" (Psalm 119:25b)

This is the first of many passionate requests found in Psalm 119, where the psalmist boldly appeals to the Source of Life to give him life!

"Give me life in your ways" (Psalm 119:37b)

"Let your mercy come to me that I may live" (Psalm 119:77a)

"In your steadfast love give me life" (Psalm 119:88a)

"Give me understanding that I may live." (Psalm 119:144b)

The author of Psalm 119 believes and declares that life is found in and through the Lord's Holy Scriptures. Similarly, Moses declared this in Deuteronomy 32:46-47:

> Take to heart all the words by which I am warning you today, that you may command them to your children, that they may be careful to do all the words of this law. For it is no empty word for you, but your very life.

What are your thoughts as you read these verses? Do you, also, believe that life is found through the Scriptures? Is the psalmist's cry for life your cry, as you go about your days? My hope and prayer is that our gracious and generous Heavenly Father will use this study to bring us all to a place of deeper conviction that the Word—the Word made flesh—is the source of "all we need for life and for godliness" (2 Peter 1:3).

" The more one studies [Psalm 119] the fresher it becomes. As those who drink the Nile water like it better every time they take a draught, so does this Psalm become the more full and fascinating the oftener you turn to it. It contains no idle word; the grapes of this cluster are almost to bursting full with the new wine of the kingdom. The more you look into this mirror of a gracious heart the more you will see in it.[1] "

The writer of Psalm 119 knows his God. He has confidence in the character of his God, even when he doesn't understand his present circumstances. The author has such an intimate relationship with his God that he freely bares his soul, humbly asks tough questions and boldly appeals for strength, grace, help, favor and ultimately life!

Studying and reflecting on the fullness of this psalm will show us that our glorious Creator and God desires to have this same intimate relationship with everyone who calls upon Him for salvation!

This Psalm is called the Alphabet of Divine Love, the Paradise of all the Doctrines, the Storehouse of the Holy Spirit, the School of Truth, also the deep mystery of the Scriptures, where the whole moral discipline of all the virtues shines brightly. And as all moral instruction is delightsome, therefore this Psalm, because excelling in this kind of instruction, should be called delightsome, inasmuch as it surpasses the rest. The other Psalms, truly, as lesser stars shine somewhat; but this burns with the meridian heat of its full brightness and is wholly resplendent with moral loveliness.[2]

Johannes Paulus Palanterius

Understanding Psalm 119

Psalm 119 is an acrostic poem divided into 22 stanzas, one for each letter of the Hebrew alphabet. It is not only the longest of all the psalms—with 176 verses, it is the longest chapter of the Bible, even longer than some of the books of the Bible. Of those 176 verses, at least 171 of them contain reference to God's Word.

Many of the saints throughout history have studied and written about this Psalm. Charles Bridges, an evangelical of the 20th century, wrote a 481-page commentary on this psalm. Thomas Manton, a prolific Puritan, wrote a three-volume work on Psalm 119, with each volume at least 500 pages!

Psalm 119 has no named author. After spending many months in this psalm, I tend to agree with Charles Spurgeon that "the hand of David is in this thing."[3] However, since no name is given, I will refer to the author as the author, writer, or psalmist.

Many of the questions throughout this study stem from the thoughts, convictions, and declarations that David Powlison shares in his article "Suffering and Psalm 119."[4]

At the outset, I encourage you to read this psalm in its entirety before beginning the study. And whenever possible, please do take time periodically to re-read the verses from previous lessons. This is certainly not a requirement, but rather a suggestion for how to gain the most benefit from this life-giving psalm. There is no danger of the text growing old!

I also recommend printing a copy of the psalm so that you can circle and underline words, phrases, and recurring themes. Use colored pencils, highlighters, pencils, and pens. Write in the margins. Interact with the text! As John Piper declares:

> 66 I know not how the light is shed,
> Nor understand this lens.
> I only know that there are eyes 99
> In pencils and in pens.[6]

"If the Writer may be permitted to suggest the method in which this Exposition may be best studied to advantage, he would beg to refer to the advice of the excellent Philip Henry to his children—that they should 'take a verse of Psalm 119 every morning to meditate upon, and so go over the Psalm twice in a year;' and 'that'— said he—'will bring you to be in love with all the rest of the Scripture.'"[5]

Cultivating Habits of Devotion

Although this psalm is about much more than spiritual practices, it is evident the psalmist lives his everyday life employing many of the spiritual disciplines in order to gain understanding of the holy and precious Word of the living God, pursuing holiness, and engaging with his faithful Lord. He exhorts us to do the same! The disciplines the psalmist uses are by no means the end goal—rather, they are some of the gracious means the Lord provides to help us learn, grow, and follow Him into deeper relationship.

> 66 The spiritual disciplines are those practices found in Scripture that promote spiritual growth among believers in the gospel of Jesus Christ. They are habits 99 of devotion, habits of experiential Christianity that have been practiced by God's people since biblical times.[7]

During the first seven chapters, we will spend a portion of time looking at one specific discipline: its definition; how it is used in this psalm; and ways in which we can grow in using this discipline (habit), with the help of the Holy Spirit, to engage with God and to love God and His Word more deeply. Chapter Eight will bring opportunities to utilize all seven of the practices.

I encourage you to incorporate these practices, or "habits of devotion," into your daily time with the Lord. Sing praise songs; choose verses or stanzas to memorize; pray through the stanzas with your own supplications.

Chapter One: Store

Chapter Two: Supplicate

Chapter Three: Study

Chapter Four: Steep

Chapter Five: Savor

Chapter Six: Surrender

Chapter Seven: Sing

Chapter Eight: Stand

The title "Psalms" comes from the Greek word *psalmois*, meaning "songs to the accompaniment of a stringed instrument."[8] Psalm 119 is a song with many genres, verses, and choruses. The song is filled with prayers of laments, questions, declarations of praise, requests, and cries for help—and that's just the beginning!

This sacred ode [Psalm 119] is a little Bible, the Scriptures condensed, a mass of Bibline, Holy Writ rewritten in holy emotions and actions. Blessed are they who can read and understand these saintly aphorisms; they shall find golden apples in this true Hesperides, and come to reckon that this Psalm, like the whole Scripture which it praises, is a pearl island, or, better still, a garden of sweet flowers.[9]

Through honest and sincere prayers of our own, and utter dependence upon the Spirit, may we grow as active and engaged students of God's living Word; lovers of God's holy, inerrant Word; and imitators of Jesus, God's Word made flesh. May we do this not out of duty, but rather out of adoration and devotion for our sovereign, righteous, and merciful God, who loves us with an everlasting, steadfast love and provided the perfect Sacrifice for our sins in His Son, Jesus Christ. "Thanks be to God for his inexpressible gift!" (2 Corinthians 9:15)

With the Helper as your guide, open your Bible, and let's enter this lush garden, full of abundant life! Look eagerly and expectantly for the sweet flowers. Inhale their fragrance. Gaze in awe at their beauty. Search for golden apples to pick, taste, and savor. May we find His words "sweet...to [our] taste" and "sweeter than honey to [our] mouths" (Psalm 119:103).

❝

I come to the garden alone,
While the dew is still on the roses,
And the voice I hear, falling on my ear,
The Son of God discloses.
And He walks with me, and He talks with me,
And He tells me I am His own,
And the joy we share as we tarry there,
None other has ever known.[10]

C. Austin Miles

❞

Chapter One

Psalm 119:1-16

"I have stored up your word in my heart, that I might not sin against you."

Psalm 119:11

 Store: *layaway; accumulate; to place or leave in a location for preservation or later use[1]*

"May the mind of Christ, my Savior,
Live in me from day to day,
By His love and power controlling
All I do and say."[2]

Kate B. Wilkinson, 1859-1928

"It [Psalm 119] is loaded with holy sense and is as weighty as it is bulky."[3]

Charles Spurgeon

Lesson One

In the Introduction, we discussed several different means or disciplines available to us to ingest the Word of God. For Chapter One, we are focusing on storing up God's Word.

>   ***Store:*** layaway; accumulate; to place or leave in a location for preservation or later use.

Read Psalm 119:1-16 slowly.

1 What are your initial thoughts and observations as we begin this journey of picking and eating what Spurgeon described as the sweet grapes of this holy, weighty psalm?

_____

_____

_____

In the first nine verses of this psalm, we are introduced to several different terms used to describe God's living and active Word. Take a minute to jot these down. As we journey through Psalm 119, we will see these terms used again and again.

_____

_____

The chart below, presented in the *ESV Study Bible*,[4] gives a specific definition for seven of the terms. If you prefer a simpler definition, all of these terms refer to God's complete spoken and written revelations.

Terms in Psalm 119 for God's Covenant Revelation

English	Hebrew	Meaning
law	*torah*	instruction
testimonies	*'edot*	what God solemnly testifies to be his will
precepts	*piqqudim*	what God has appointed to be done
statutes	*khuqqim; khuqqot*	what the divine Lawgiver has laid down
commandments	*mitswot*	what God has commanded
rules	*mishpatim*	what the divine Judge has ruled to be right
word	*imrah; dabar*	what God has spoken

2 Read through verses 1-16 again, paying attention to the psalmist's attitudes and actions towards God's Word. His attitudes aren't always specifically spelled out for us, but what attitudes do you pick up on as you read his requests? What specific actions does he take or intend to take?

Attitudes: _____   *Actions:* _____

_____   _____

_____   _____

_____   _____

_____   _____

3 As we begin this study, take the opportunity to reflect on the following questions:

Which of these attitudes do you desire to have towards God's Word?

_____

_____

_____

Which of the psalmist's actions would you most like to imitate?

_____

_____

_____

In what specific ways would you like to grow in loving, following and delighting in His Word? For example, maybe you desire that your days and lips be more regularly full of praises to your God? v.7 or, from v.15, maybe you'd like to spend more intentional time meditating on God's Holy Word?

_____

_____

_____

_____

4 Compose a personal prayer to the LORD, using exact words/verses from this section of Psalm 119, sharing with Him your desires and requests.

> For as the rain and the snow come down from heaven and do not return there but water the earth, making it bring forth and sprout, giving seed to the sower and bread to the eater, so shall my word be that goes out from my mouth; it shall not return to me empty, but it shall accomplish that which I purpose, and shall succeed in the thing for which I sent it.

Isaiah 55:10-11

"Blessed be the name of the LORD from this time forth and forevermore!
From the rising of the sun to its setting, the name of the LORD is to be praised!"

Psalm 113:2-3

"Blessed is he who comes in the name of the Lord!"

Luke 13:35

Lesson Two

Read Psalm 119:1-16.

Verses 1-3 serve as an introduction to the psalm.

1 What are the defining characteristics/actions of the blessed from these three verses?

_____

_____

_____

What is the specific desire the psalmist expresses in verse 5?_____

_____

_____

2 What hope does the psalmist (along with all believers) have of keeping all the statutes of our God and walking blamelessly before Him?

_____

_____

First, the bad news: **Read Romans 3:9-12** and put into your own words:

_____

_____

_____

_____

In our own strength, we cannot hope to do no wrong or seek God with our whole hearts. But here's the good news:

66 But when the goodness and loving kindness of God our Savior appeared, he 99
saved us, not because of works done by us in righteousness, but according to
his own mercy… (Titus 3:4-5)

3 The Holy Scriptures tell us there is only ONE whose way is blameless, who sought the Lord with His whole heart. How is this Holy One described in the following passages?

Hebrews 4:15 _____

_____

_____

_____

Hebrews 5:7-10 _____

_____

_____

_____

Although the specific name of Jesus is not mentioned in the book of Psalms, the psalms are FULL of His story and presence!

Luke 24:44 says,

> 66   Then he [Jesus] said to them, 'These are my words that I spoke to you while I was still with you, that everything written about me in the Law of Moses and the Prophets and the Psalms must be fulfilled.'   99

Writing about that verse, Tremper Longman III says, "Jesus' language [here] makes it absolutely certain that he believed the Psalms anticipated his future ministry of suffering and glory."[5]

At the very start of Psalm 119, we see a beautiful picture of Jesus, the only one whose way is blameless, who walked perfectly in the ways of the Lord. Throughout this psalm, let's be on the lookout for Jesus, the one who "himself has suffered when tempted" (Heb 2:18), "yet without sin" (Heb 4:15).

4   The following passages declare the amazing truth, hope, and good news for those who place their faith in Jesus! Read these passages and jot down the key points from each:

Romans 3:21-26 ....

....

....

Romans 5:6-11, 18-21 ....

....

....

Titus 2:11-14 ....

....

....

God takes a heart in which righteousness does not exist, speaks the Word of life, and where once there was nothing, there is something; the righteousness of Christ. Where there was no righteousness, now there is his righteousness.[6]

Because of His great love for us, through the sacrificial death of His beloved Son, God has provided a way for us to be one of his blameless, declared-righteous, dearly beloved children! Jesus knew we would never "do no wrong" while living on this earth, so He obeyed *for* us, in *our* place.

Once we confess our sin, repent, and surrender our lives to Him, we become one of the blameless ones! When our merciful Father looks at us, He sees the sacrifice and perfection of His Son, Jesus.

> I will greatly rejoice in the LORD; my soul shall exult in my God, for he has clothed me with the garments of salvation; he has covered me with the robe of righteousness (Isaiah 61:10a)

5 Take a few minutes to reflect on these amazing truths and offer a prayer of praise to the Lord for His incredible kindness to you through Jesus!

_____

_____

_____

_____

_____

_____

_____

"Scripture has power that is supernatural, soothing, convicting, transforming, life-changing, timely, timeless, and eternal. Nothing beats having the Word of God stored away in the chambers of the mind." [7]

Robert J. Morgan

"I have stored up your word in my heart, that I might not sin against you."

Psalm 119:11

"When we memorize a word, phrase, line, or verse from God's Word, it's like implanting a powerful radioactive speck of the very mind of God into our own finite brains. As we learn it "by heart," it descends into the hidden crevices and fissures of our souls. As we meditate on it, it begins sending out its quiet, therapeutic waves of influence." [8]

Robert J. Morgan

Lesson Three

Robert J. Morgan, an author and pastor, has written the book *100 Bible Verses Everyone Should Know by Heart.* He says this about storing, our focus for this lesson:

> 66 Remember, whenever we store away a verse in our minds, it becomes a concealed weapon. It's a light, a lamp, a vault of gold, a hive of honey, and a two-edged sword. It's available day and night for practical purposes. It helps us "fix" our thoughts, and we fix our thoughts by fixing them on Jesus via His praiseworthy Word.[9] 99

1 Take a look at the following passages and then answer the questions.

Proverbs 7:1-3

These verses list specific actions we are to take regarding the Word. What do you think the author meant by each of these phrases?

"Keep my teaching as the apple of your eye"

_____

_____

"Bind them on your fingers"
_____

_____

_____

"Write them on the tablet of your heart" _____

_____

_____

_____

John 15:1-7

Here's the definition of abide: to remain stable or fixed in a state. According to this verse, why is it important to have God's word abiding in us?

_____

_____

Colossians 3:16

Think of someone you know personally who has God's Word "dwelling" in them "richly." In what specific ways does this make a difference in their everyday life?

_____

_____

_____

Before we finish this section, think about this translation of Deuteronomy 6:4-7a from the Contemporary English Version: "Listen, Israel! The LORD our God is the only true God! So love the LORD your God with all your heart, soul, and strength. *Memorize* his laws and tell them to your children over and over again" (emphasis added).

Jeremiah 31:33

Who does the writing?_____

_____

_____

> When you memorize biblical texts, you're putting frames around the verses and hanging them on the walls of your inner library. And you'll find as you visualize them that you're always in the picture.[10]
>
> **Robert J. Morgan**

We can do the memorizing, but we are completely dependent upon God and His Spirit to "fix them" or "write them" on our hearts and minds in a way that has an effect on our daily living.

2 In Psalm 119:11, the psalmist is declaring that storing up the Word in his heart and mind will keep him from sinning. Consider trying an experiment while you go through this study. Take some time with the Lord and ask for His thoughts. What is a habitual sin in your life? If you have trouble thinking of one, ask your spouse or close friend for input! Find one or two verses or short Bible passages that present specific truths that help motivate you to fight against this sin. Begin to commit these verses to memory. Be on the lookout to see how the Lord uses these stored truths to help you in your battle against sin and temptation.

3 **Read and pray through 119:1-16.** Use specific verses to share with the Lord your desire to walk in His statutes, store up His Word, and delight in His ways. Thank Him for specific gifts found in His Word.

*"Blessed is the man who trusts in the L*ORD*, whose trust is the L*ORD*.*
He is like a tree planted by water, that sends out its roots by the
stream, and does not fear when heat comes, for its leaves remain green,
and is not anxious in the year of drought, for it does not
cease to bear fruit."

Jeremiah 17:7-8

"The grass withers, the flower fades,
but the word of our God will stand forever."

Isaiah 40:8

Lesson Four

Read Psalm 119:1-16 and Psalm 1

1 What connections and similarities do you see between these two passages?

_____

_____

_____

_____

The lush and flowering tree in Psalm 1 is a beautiful picture of the person who delights in and meditates on the Word of God. Throughout Psalm 119, we will see this overarching theme:

The one who knows, follows, and delights in God and His Word, although not promised a life free of suffering, will live a fruitful and an abundant life, both here on the earth and in heaven for all eternity.

There is supreme value and abundant blessing in knowing, obeying, and delighting in God's Word. In fact, our very lives—both while on this earth and for all eternity—are dependent upon this life-giving Word!

2 To see additional blessings promised to those who love and follow God's ways, look up the following passages and answer these questions for each passage:

Deuteronomy 5:28-6:3 and 6:17-19

What are the specific blessings mentioned?

_____

_____

Who will receive the blessings?

_____

_____

3 The Bible contains well over 1000 pages, and it's filled with instructions and commands. How can we possibly remember and obey all the Bible's commandments? Exactly what *are* the commandments we are to fix our eyes on and obey?

The following passages show us where to begin. Take some time to read and reflect on what the Lord is asking of His chosen people—both the Israelites and His followers today.

Deuteronomy 6:4-9

Matthew 22:36-40

Mark 12:28-31

John 15:12-17

Which commands does Jesus say are most important?

_____

_____

4   Take time for reflection and dialogue with your Lord and Savior.

How does He want you to grow in loving Him with all your heart, mind, and soul?

_____

_____

_____

Are you aware of other things or people that you are loving more than God?

_____

_____

_____

5   Take time to pray. Declare your utter dependence upon God to help you love Him with all that you are. Confess and repent of specific ways you haven't been loving God or people as much as you love yourself. Thank Him for the precious, undeserved gift of His forgiveness.

_____

_____

_____

_____

_____

_____

"Someone once told me that Scripture memory accelerates the transformation process in our lives. It's like a special additive that exponentially increases the efficiency of sanctification. By internalizing Bible verses, we're mainstreaming God's thoughts into our conscious, subconscious, and unconscious logic." [11]

Robert J. Morgan

"What a fool I have been, to lie like this in a stinking dungeon, when I could have just as well walked free. In my chest pocket I have a key called Promise that will, I am thoroughly persuaded, open any lock in Doubting-Castle." [12]

John Bunyan, *Pilgrim's Progress*

"When I discovered your words, I devoured them. They are my joy and my heart's delight, for I bear your name, O LORD, God of Heaven's armies."

Jeremiah 15:16 NLT

Lesson Five

Read 119:1-16

Starting with verse 4, the psalmist begins a heartfelt prayer to his LORD that continues throughout the psalm. David Powlison explains the psalm this way:

> Psalm 119 is a personal prayer. It's where I go to learn utter and utterly appropriate honesty. I learn how to open my heart about what matters, to the person I most trust. It's relentless, not repetitive. It's personal, not propositional: Lord, you spoke. You acted. I need You. Make me into what You say I should be. Do what You say You'll do. I love You. [13]

1 Circle the many requests the psalmist asks of God in these first two stanzas.

It is obvious that the author recognizes his need for divine help to obey. He knows he can't keep the Lord's precepts in his own strength. Here's how I would say verses 5 and 8: "I am trying to, oh, how I want to keep your statutes; but I often don't. Please, Lord, do not utterly forsake me!" The psalmist is one of us. He is a fellow sinner who wants to do right, but often doesn't. *How does he deal with this frustration in his prayer?*

_____

_____

_____

2   What words/attitudes describe the author's understanding of his weaknesses and his dependence on God's help to grow in obedience?

_____

_____

_____

_____

3   Paul describes this very tension between our flesh and godly desires in Romans 7. **Read Romans 7:15-8:11.**

In what specific ways can you relate? _____

_____

_____

_____

From this passage in Romans, write down specific graces and hopes that are available to you as a believer and follower of Jesus Christ:

_____

_____

_____

Each verse in Psalm 119: 9-16 begins with the second letter of the Hebrew alphabet, *beth*. The word *beth* also means "a house." Herbert Lockyer notes, "The underlying thought of the stanza is ... making our heart a home for the Word of God."[14]

You may be familiar with the booklet *My Heart: Christ's Home*, written in 1951 by Robert Boyd Munger, a Presbyterian minister. Following is an excerpt to help us consider this concept of "making our heart a home for the Word of God."

"We walked next into the living room. This room was rather intimate and comfortable. I liked it. It had a fireplace, overstuffed chairs, a sofa, and a quiet atmosphere. He, (Christ) also seemed pleased with it. He said, "This is indeed a delightful room. Let us come here often. It is secluded and quiet, and we can fellowship together." Well, naturally as a young Christian I was thrilled. I couldn't think of anything I would rather do than have a few minutes with Christ in intimate companionship. He promised, "I will be here early every morning. Meet me here, and we will start the day together." So, morning after morning, I would come downstairs to the living room and He would take a book of the Bible from the bookcase. He would open it and then we would read together. He would tell me of its riches and unfold to me its truths. He would make my heart warm as He revealed His love and His grace He had toward me. These were wonderful hours together. In fact, we called the living room the "withdrawing room." It was a period when we had our quiet time together. But, little by little, under the pressure of many responsibilities, this time began to be shortened. Why, I don't know, but I thought I was just too busy to spend time with Christ. This was not intentional, you understand; it just happened that way. Finally, not only was the time shortened, but I began to miss a day now and then. It was examination time at the university. Then it was some other urgent emergency. I would miss it two days in a row and often more.

As I passed the living room, the door was open. Looking in, I saw a fire in the fireplace and Jesus was sitting there. Suddenly in dismay I thought to myself, "He was my guest. I invited Him into my heart! He has come as Lord of my home. And yet here I am neglecting Him." I turned and went in. With downcast glance, I said, "Blessed Master, forgive me. Have You been here all these mornings?" "Yes," He said, "I told you I would be here every morning to meet with you." Then I was even more ashamed. He had been faithful in spite of my faithlessness. I asked His forgiveness and He readily forgave me as He does when we are truly repentant. "The trouble with you is this: you have been thinking of the quiet time, of the Bible study and prayer time, as a factor in your own spiritual progress, but you have forgotten that this hour means something to me also. Remember, I love you. I have redeemed you at great cost. I value your fellowship. Now," He said, "do not neglect this hour if only for my sake. Whatever else may be your desire, remember I want your fellowship!" You know, the truth that Christ desires my companionship, that He loves me, wants me to be with Him, wants to be with me and waits for me, has done more to transform my quiet time with God than any other single fact. Don't let Christ wait alone in the living room of your heart, but every day find some time when, with your Bible and in prayer, you may be together with Him."[15]

4 Take some time to seek the Lord's perspective and answer the following questions:

How does my Savior want me to grow in making my heart a home for the living Word of God?

_____

_____

What steps can I take to store up God's Word in my heart? _____

_____

_____

Ask the Lord to search your heart. Confess specific ways you have disobeyed and not kept His precepts diligently. Are there specific areas of your life where you are conveniently forgetting His Word and doing things your own way?

_____

_____

_____

_____

Is there specific sin that is hardening your heart toward God and/or His Word or causing you to wander from His commandments? Is there an area of life where you are making a habit of disobeying His Word? If so, seize the opportunity to repent, and then receive the forgiveness and cleansing that our gracious Savior promises to those who humble themselves and confess.

If we confess our sins, He is faithful and just to forgive us our sins and to cleanse us from all unrighteousness.

1 John 1:9

Whoever conceals his transgressions will not prosper, but he who confesses and forsakes them will obtain mercy.

Proverbs 28:13

_____

_____

_____

_____

5 To conclude Chapter One, I encourage you to choose one or more verses from 1-16 to memorize. Write out the verse(s) and begin committing these words to memory. As we continue through Psalm 119, please also consider choosing one or more stanzas to hide in your heart. If you are completing this study with your small group, ask the others in your group to join you. This could be a perfect time for some friendly competition and motivation!

https://www.desiringgod.org/articles/five-tips-for-bible-memory

Chapter Two

Psalm 119:17-40

*Open my eyes, that I may behold
wonderful things out of your law.*

Psalm 119:18

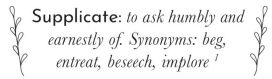

Supplicate: *to ask humbly and
earnestly of. Synonyms: beg,
entreat, beseech, implore* [1]

*"If you ever longed for a life of deep and fruitful prayer,
give yourself to the Word of God. Read it. Think about it.
Memorize it. Be shaped by it."* [2]

John Piper

*"As we seek the living God through His living Word,
He makes Himself available to us."* [3]

Mike Bullmore

Lesson One

During this lesson we will look at the second discipline, supplication.

Supplicate: ask or beg for something earnestly or humbly.

Psalm 119 is abounding with supplications! In this lesson, we'll look at what specific things the psalmist earnestly begs God to do for him. We'll ask what we can learn about prayer, or supplications, from listening in and interacting with the author's humble pleas.

In growing to understand this psalm and write this study, I have found David Powlison's article "Suffering and Psalm 119" to be instructive. I am including several quotes from him throughout this lesson. I encourage you to refer back to his thoughts often, as we continue searching for gold in Psalm 119.

> Psalm 119 is the most extensive I-to-You conversation in the Bible. We hear what a man says out loud in God's presence; his joyous pleasure, vocal need, open adoration, blunt requests, candid assertions, deep struggles, fiercely good intentions; it's an outcry of faith.[4]

1 **Read verses 119: 17-40** and circle the many different blunt and passionate requests the psalmist makes of the Lord.

There are 9 requests in verses 33-40 alone, with several more in verses 17-32. Notice the numerous I-You references. Write down two or more of the psalmist's requests that you, also, desire to ask of God.

2 What are the psalmist's reasons for making these requests? In other words, what are the benefits he is hoping to receive? (v.17, 18, 27, 33, 34)

_____

_____

_____

66   The plain, fluent words you overhear in Psalm 119 spring from a man already persuaded. He simply talks, fusing his intellect, will, emotions, circumstances, desires, fears, needs, memory, and anticipation. He's keenly aware of what he's really like. He's keenly aware of what's happening to him. He's keenly aware of the LORD and the relevance of what the LORD sees, says, and does. Such awareness makes him very direct and very personal. The living heart of a man tumbles out in passionate requests and passionate affirmations. He persuades us not by argument, but by infectious, vocal faith.[5]   99

David Powlinson

I believe that prayer is the measure of the man, spiritually, in a way that nothing else is, so that how we pray is as important a question as we can ever face.[6]

J.I. Packer

3 Let's consider what we learn about the psalmist from listening in on his prayers.

What are the psalmist's fears/concerns? (v.19, 25, 31)

_____

_____

_____

*How would you describe the emotions expressed?*_____

_____

_____

_____

What does the psalmist want God to "remove" or "take away"? (v.22, 29, 37, 39)

_____

_____

_____

What are his affirmations/declarations about God? His Word? (v.18, 23, 24, 25, 28)

_____

_____

4 Using verses or phrases from 17-40, write out a personal, honest prayer to the Lord, sharing your fears, concerns, and requests. Declare who God is and what is true about His character and His Word.

_____

_____

_____

_____

5 Spend a few moments storing up the verses or passages you have chosen to hide in your heart.

"O God, hear my prayer;
Give ear to the words of my mouth."

Psalm 54:2

"Q: What is prayer?

A: Prayer is an offering up of our desires unto God,
For things agreeable to his will, in the name of Christ,
With confession of our sins,
And thankful acknowledgment of his mercies."[7]

Westminster Shorter Catechism, question 98

"In the days of his flesh, Jesus offered up prayers and supplications,
with loud cries and tears, to him who was able to save him from death"

Hebrews 5:7

Lesson Two

Psalm 119 is the thoughtful outcry that rises when real life meets real God. A person who has listened opens his heart to the Person who has spoken. Psalm 119 gets you about the business of a living dialogue with the Person whose opinion finally matters.[8]

1 Read Psalm 119:17-40.

In a sentence or two, how would you describe the psalmist's circumstances? _____

_____

_____

In what ways does the author allow his circumstances to intersect with specific truths from the breathing, living Word?

_____

_____

Where, specifically, does the psalmist believe he will find hope and life? _____

_____

_____

Take some time to think about your prayer life. Are you familiar with the psalmist's way of praying, or does it seem foreign to you? Do you think about prayer with a sense of guilt or condemnation, knowing you should pray, but struggling to do so? Write down a few reflections you have about your prayer life.

_____

_____

_____

2 Let's take a look at how Jesus prioritized prayer while He walked on the earth, fully God yet fully Man. Then answer the following questions.

Matthew 26:36-44

Mark 1:29-35; 6:30-46

Luke 5:15-16; 6:6-12

Hebrews 5:7

*What were some of the circumstances when Jesus prayed?*_____

_____

_____

*What were His cries when His real life met His real God?*_____

_____

_____

*What emotions did Jesus express while praying?*_____

_____

In what ways does the psalmist imitate Jesus while praying?

What affected you the most from these passages about how Jesus prayed?

How does the fact that Jesus intentionally made time to pray change or deepen your desire to pray? If Jesus needed to pray, what does that say about us?

Do you have a consistent plan for getting away to pray? I encourage you to be ruthless and creative in scheduling regular times to engage and fellowship with your Savior and Shepherd. This could mean setting your alarm half an hour earlier one or more days per week. For moms of little ones, you might consider trading babysitting with a fellow mom and spending a couple of hours with your journal and Bible at a local coffee shop. An overnight at a local retreat center, or a specific day of the week set aside for extended Bible/prayer time could be a great option for women in any season of life!

Even if frequent times of getting away isn't an option for you in this season of life, consider the heart and actions of Susanna Wesley, the mother of 19 children in the early 1700s. Although not able to get off by herself in the midst of such a busy household, Susanna often threw her apron over her head. Her children knew not to disturb her, as this was her time to pray and engage with the Lord!

Take some extended time to pray today. What fears, requests, and praises would you like to share with the Lord as you consider how your real life meets with your real God?

What relevant truths has God spoken in His Word that can bring perspective and hope to your present situation?

_____

_____

_____

_____

Have a living dialogue with the One who created you and chose you before time began, the One who loves you with "an everlasting love"(Jeremiah 31:3).

_____

_____

_____

_____

"And he told them a parable to the effect that they ought always to pray and not lose heart."

Luke 18:1

"Psalm 119 is not information about the Bible, it's speech therapy for the inarticulate."[9]

David Powlison

"O Father of glory, this is the cry of our hearts-to be changed from one degree of glory to another, until, in the resurrection, at the last trumpet, we are completely conformed to the image of your Son, Jesus Christ, our Lord. Until then, we long to grow in grace and in the knowledge of our Lord, especially the knowledge of his glory. We want to see it as clearly as we see the sun, and to savor it as deeply as our most desired pleasure."[10]

John Piper

Lesson Three

1 Today, take time to go back to the beginning and **read Psalm 119:1-40**, paying
attention to the different requests or prayers the psalmist makes regarding his eyes.

*What does the psalmist want to fix his eyes on?*_____

_____

*What does he want the Lord to do with his eyes?*_____

_____

In verse 18, the author asks the Lord to open his eyes. The Hebrew word used here for
the verb "open" is the same word used in the story of Balaam in Numbers 22:31, when
"the LORD opened the eyes of Balaam" so that he could see "the angel of the LORD standing in the way, with his drawn sword."

(If you have time, check out this real-life Dr. Doolittle story in Numbers 22. If our God
can make a donkey speak, He can certainly hear our prayers!)

The psalmist understands his desperate need for the Lord's help to understand, value and
obey God's Word. He knows with certainty that unless the Lord removes the veil from his
cloudy, dull eyes, he will never see the awesome glory of God or the wondrous things in
His Holy Word.

What does the author ask the Lord to turn his eyes away from in verse 37? _____

_____

_____

_____

John Bunyan refers to this verse in his book *Pilgrim's Progress*. While Christian and Faithful are making their way to the Celestial City, they come to a yearlong event called Vanity Fair, where "pleasures and delights of all sorts" are sold. The two pilgrims had no interest in looking upon these wares. If asked to buy something, "they would put their fingers in their ears, and cry, 'Turn away mine eyes from beholding vanity', and look upwards, signifying that their trade and traffic was in heaven." When asked what they would like to buy, the pilgrims answered, "We buy the truth."[11]

2 A few questions to ponder:

Am I gazing at worthless things that are:

> *hardening my heart towards God?*
> *dulling my hunger for spiritual food?*
> *hindering me from spending time in the Word and prayer?* _____

_____

_____

_____

According to verse 37, what is the opposite of "experiencing life"? _____

_____

_____

_____

*Where does life come from according to verses 25, 37, 40?*_____

_____

_____

3 In Luke 11:34-36, what is the sober truth Jesus teaches us regarding our eyes?

_____

_____

_____

4 **Read Psalm 121 and 123** and notice the many times eyes are mentioned. How should we look? Where should we look?

_____

_____

_____

_____

5 To see what our Lord's eyes look upon, check out these verses. Remember that as surrendered believers in Jesus, God covers us with the blameless, spotless blood of His Son. Jesus clothes us with His robe of righteousness. Hallelujah!

2 Chronicles 16:9

1 Peter 3:12

1 Corinthians 2:9

Think back to the most incredibly beautiful places you have seen with your own eyes, either in person or in a picture. Offer a shout of praise to the Lord for the promise of what your eyes will behold in the future!

What specific truth from Scripture—and/or which of God's attributes—would it help to gaze upon today as you consider your current emotions, circumstances, desires, fears, and needs?

_____

_____

_____

_____

6 Compose a prayer, asking the Lord to fix your eyes on these specific truths. Confess and repent of any ways you are looking at worthless things. Thank Him for specific ways He has His eyes on you.

_____

_____

_____

_____

_____

_____

_____

"Speak, O God, through your written Word
with stone-cleaving power,
and grant us to see the truth of Jesus everywhere.
Bend our affections toward him."[12]

John Piper

"Prayer is my chief work; by it I carry on all else.
Prayer is the nearest approach to God and the highest enjoyment
of him that we are capable of in this life. It is the noblest
exercise of the soul. It is the most exalted use of our best faculties.
It is the highest imitation of the blessed beings of heaven."[13]

William Law (1686-1761)

Lesson Four

1 Read Psalm 119:17-40.

How does the psalmist respond to the painful realities of scorn, sorrow, reproach, and loneliness?

_____

_____

Do these feelings turn the psalmist inward toward himself (self-pity), downward into despair, or upward?

_____

_____

What specific phrases help you come to this conclusion? _____

_____

_____

2 The psalmist is "laid low" (v. 25) and "melting away in sorrow" (v. 28), yet he makes Godward choices. Record the deliberate actions he takes in these stanzas. A few examples are found in verses 23, 24, 30-32.

_____

_____

Notice the author's declaration in verse 26. He talks with the Lord about his ways (actions). He lays it all out on the table. The King James version translates v.26 like this: "I have declared my ways, and thou heardest me: teach me thy statutes."

In his "Exposition of Psalm 119" Charles Bridges says this about v. 26:

66   A beautiful description of the 'simplicity and godly sincerity' of the believer's 'walk with God'! He spreads his whole case before his God, *'declaring his ways'* of sinfulness, of difficulty, and of conduct. And, indeed, it is our privilege to acquaint our Father with all our care and need, that we may be pitied by His love, and guided by His counsel, and confirmed by His strength. Who would not find relief by unbosoming himself to his Father? This showing of ourselves to God—*declaring our ways* of sin before Him without deceit—is the short and sure way of rest.[14]   99

Consider this explanation from David Powlison, pertaining to the psalm as a whole, but certainly true of this specific verse:

66   Psalm 119 is about life's painful realities. And it is about the gifts of God. And it is about how those two meet, talk, come to grips, and find life's highest delight.   99

4 **Read 1 Peter 2:18-25** and reflect on our Savior's response to His suffering.

What were Jesus' painful realities? _____

_____

_____

How do the gifts of God meet and make a difference in Jesus' painful realities?

Now look back at verses 119:17-40.

What are the "painful realities" David is facing?

What "gifts of God" are presented in our text?

How do David's "painful realities" intersect with God's gifts?

5 To end our time today, talk with the Lord. Spread your whole case before Him. In humility, cry out with "blunt requests". Speak His truth back to Him, reflecting on how the truth of God's character and His promises intersect with your personal realities. With thanksgiving, declare "open adoration" for His steadfast love and the gift of salvation.

_____

_____

_____

_____

_____

_____

_____

_____

_____

6 Spend a few minutes working on your memory verses from Chapter One.

"In the end the Christian life is a life of being carried from beginning to end. We work. 'But it is not we, but God who works within us.' (1 Corinthians 15:10)" [16]

John Piper

"Let us hold unswervingly to the hope we profess, for he who promised is faithful."

Hebrews 10:23 (NIV)

"Since beginning the day with the Word of God is crucial, therefore prayer is equally crucial since the Word will not open its best wonders to us without prayer." [17]

John Piper

Lesson Five

1 **Read Psalm 119:17-40**, and then circle or highlight the three times the psalmist refers to his heart.

In order to love and obey God with all his heart, what does the psalmist know needs to happen? (v.32, 34, 36)

_____

_____

The psalmist declares that he can only run in the way of the Lord's commandments *when* the Lord enlarges his heart!

Here is how the ESV Study Bible describes "enlarge my heart":

> Or "make my heart broad"; cf. I Kings 4:29, where "breadth of heart or mind" is an expanded ability to perceive God's truth.[18]

Charles Spurgeon gives this commentary on verse 32 (emphasis mine):

> "Yes, the heart is the master; the feet soon run when the heart is free and energetic. Let the affections be aroused and eagerly set on divine things, and our actions will be full of force, swiftness, and delight. *God must work in us first,* and then we shall will and do according to his good pleasure. *He must change* the heart, unite the heart, encourage the heart, strengthen the heart, and enlarge the heart, and then the course of the life will be gracious, sincere,

happy, and earnest; so that from our lowest up to our highest state in grace *we must attribute* all to the free favor of our God."[19]

Through the psalmist's "vocal need, open adoration, blunt requests, candid assertions, deep struggles, fiercely good intentions,"[20] we are made aware of the ongoing inter-changes operating in his life (and the life of every follower of Jesus). God's Word is filled with promises of ways He will meet us, help us, and change us. His Word also contains exhortations and commandments for specific actions we are to take in order to be obedi-ent. We can only take these actions with the help of His Spirit, the Helper. There is such mystery here that we will only scratch the surface! However, for the remainder of today's lesson, we will look at a few of the specific things God promises to do in the life of every believer, as well as what our responsibilities are as members of His family.

In modern language, the psalmist's prayer might sound like this:

66 Lord, from reading Your Word I know I am to run toward You and Your Kingdom ways. I want to run; but I so often walk with a limp, fall down, or even sinfully run in the opposite direction. I acknowledge that I cannot begin to run toward You, toward obedience, toward understanding and delight, without Your divine, immediate, and constant help! Please, dear God, change my heart; unite my heart; enlarge my heart! 99

2 **Read 17-40** and fill in the chart considering this question: what actions does the *psalmist* commit to do and what does the psalmist ask *God* to do?

*Lord, I can only do this:*_____   *If/when You do this:*_____

3 Take a look at a few other passages that highlight this ongoing interchange between God's faithful actions and our responsibilities:

Philippians 2:12-13

Ephesians 3:20

Philippians 1:6

Hebrews 13:20-21

In your own words, how would you describe the things God promises to do for us and the things He asks us to do when it comes to growing in godliness?

_____

_____

_____

_____

4 Compose a prayer to the Lord, using verses 33-40 as your guide. Ask Him to teach you something specific. Plead with Him for understanding about a certain spiritual topic. Humbly request His leading in a particular circumstance. Declare your dependence and desire that He incline your heart toward a specific obedience.

Let this truth from 1 Thessalonians 5:23 fill your heart and mind with hope and faith, as you bring your requests before Him:

66 Now may the God of peace himself sanctify you completely, and may your whole spirit and soul and body be kept blameless at the coming of our Lord Jesus Christ. He who calls you is faithful; he will surely do it. 99

Father, teach me: _____

_____

_____

*Give me understanding in:*_____

_____

_____

*Lead me in this situation:*_____

_____

_____

Incline my heart toward obedience in this area: _____

_____

_____

*Thank you for:*_____

_____

_____

5 Select one or more verses from this chapter to store up. Spend time committing verses from Chapters One and Two to memory.

Chapter Three

Psalm 119:41-88

*"You are good and do good;
teach me your statutes."*

Psalm 119:68

Study: *to read in detail especially
with the intention of learning; to
consider attentively or in detail.*[3]

"Oh, help our unbelief.
Incline our hearts to your Word and to its assurances that you
"work all things according to the counsel of your will…"[1]

John Piper

"May the Word of God dwell richly
In my heart from hour to hour,
So that all may see I triumph
Only through His power." [2]

Kate B. Wilkinson, 1859-1928

"In humility receive the word implanted, which is able to save your souls…"

James 1:21 (NASB)

Lesson One

Read Psalm 119:41-88.

1 What words would you use to describe the attitudes and emotions of the psalmist?

_____

_____

_____

_____

2 Find and highlight, or circle, the three specific verses where the psalmist asks God to teach him something. Look back also at verses 12, 26, 29, and 33. By the end of this psalm, we will see in ten different verses how the psalmist asks God to "teach him." He is teachable and desiring to learn from the One "in whom are hidden all the treasures of wisdom and knowledge" (Colossians 2:3). The psalmist is a student of God's commandments, declaring his utter need for God's help not only to understand the commandments, but to obey the commandments in his daily thoughts, convictions, and actions.

3 Look up the following verses to see the importance the Lord places on humility and a teachable spirit. Rewrite them in your own words.

Psalm 51:17 _____

_____

Isaiah 57:15 _____

_____

Isaiah 66 1-:2 _____

_____

The Lord blesses the humble and teachable. There is no greater example of humility than our Lord and Savior, Jesus Christ.

4 **Read Philippians 2:3-11** and record specific words or actions that describe Jesus' heart of humility.

_____

_____

_____

Notice the hope and truth for believers declared in verse 5. How and why is humility attainable for followers of Jesus?

_____

_____

_____

5 Compose a prayer to Jesus, specifically thanking Him for His humility. Confess any ways you have been proud towards Him or others. Ask for the help of the Holy Spirit to grow in developing a teachable, humble spirit, using one or more of the verses or passages from today's readings.

"Take away the Word and you deprive us of the sun." [4]

Martin Luther

"How firm a foundation, ye saints of the Lord,
Is laid for your faith in His excellent Word!
What more can He say than to you He hath said,
To you who for refuge to Jesus have fled?" [5]

"K" in Rippon's Selection, 1787

"Psalm 119 opens doors into the rest of Scripture.
Old friends become better friends." [6]

David Powlison

Lesson Two

Our spiritual discipline focus during Chapter Three is "*Study:* to read in detail especially with the intention of learning; to consider attentively or in detail".

Let's discover just how important it is that we regularly devote time and attention to studying God's Word.

1 **Read Ezra 7:7-11** and notice how Ezra, the priest, is described. What is the reason for "God's good hand to be upon him"?

_____

_____

2 Using the passages below, complete the following statements:

Psalm 119:89   *God's Word is:* _____

Isaiah 40:8   _____

Isaiah 55:10-11   _____

2 Timothy 3:14-17   _____

Hebrews 4:12   _____

1 Peter 1:23-25   _____

Psalm 119:25   *God's Word can satisfy me in these ways:* _____

Psalm 119:107   _____

Psalm 119:156   _____

Isaiah 55:1-3   _____

Matthew 4:4   _____

John 6:35   _____

In the beginning was the Word, and the Word was with God, and the Word was God. He was in the beginning with God...In him was life...

John 1:1-2, 4a

God's Word leads us to Christ, Who leads us to *life!* The pleas and declarations found in Psalm 119 give us a powerful picture of someone who recognizes his desperate need for the life-giving elements found in the Word.

3 Record the declarations and requests for life found in Psalm 119:50, 77, and 88, as well as these previous verses: 25, 37, and 40.

Declarations: _____   *Requests:* _____

_____   _____

_____   _____

_____   _____

_____   _____

According to these verses, where are the places abundant life is found?

_____

_____

4 Read Acts 8:26-40 and record the actions and attitudes of this Ethiopian student towards the Scriptures:

Attitudes: _____   *Actions:* _____

_____   _____

_____   _____

_____   _____

_____   _____

Consider Justin Taylor's thoughts regarding this passage of Scripture in this excerpt from his article "A Teachable Spirit":

> To be sure, this is a historical narrative recounting an event. The purpose is not necessarily to guide believers today in how to read their Bibles or how to think about the teaching of God's Word. But the elements within it nonetheless correspond to some wise principles we can adopt as our own. So let's work through the passage again, letting the various points serve as triggers for our own reflection on understanding the Word of God and those who teach it.
>
> First, the Ethiopian wrestles with and labors to understand the meaning of God's Word. He doesn't wait for help; he first tries on his own to figure out what the text is saying. He is not content merely to skim the Scriptures, putting a check mark next to his reading in the scroll for that day. And so it is with us — we must spend time in the Bible, working hard and trusting God for insight into its meaning. Paul expressed this as a command followed by a promise: "Think over what I say, for the Lord will give you understanding in everything" (2 Tim. 2:7).
>
> Second, the eunuch humbly acknowledges his own insufficiency and lack of understanding. He desires to understand what the Word says, he admits that he needs help, and then he asks for it. We should approach God first remembering that He wants to be asked and that He promises to assist us: "If any of you lacks wisdom, let him ask God, who gives generously to all without reproach, and it will be given him" (James 1:5). And what should we pray?

Psalm 119 provides many examples of how to pray for understanding. For example, verses 64, 66, and 68 say, "Teach me…," and verse 73 says, "Give me understanding that I may learn…" Taylor continues,

> Third, the eunuch asks a good, clear, relevant question based upon his own wrestling with the meaning of the text. Asking good questions is evidence of good thinking. If you don't ask good questions about the text, you won't engage your mind and you won't be able to evaluate the answers.
>
> Fourth, he listens carefully to the Christ-centered, gospel-focused teaching before him. Jesus warned that we must take care how we listen (Luke 8:18), and the Ethiopian eunuch does just that. For many of us, our inclination is to talk first and listen second, but Christ-followers must be "quick to hear" and "slow to speak" (James 1:19).
>
> Finally, he puts into practice what he has just learned from the Word and from his commentator. Philip had told him "the good news about Jesus" (Acts 8:35), which probably included the teaching that members of God's covenant community will publicly identify with Christ in the act of baptism. So the Ethiopian official models for us James' command to "be doers of the word, and not hearers only" (James 1:22).
>
> So let us be the sort of people who prayerfully and carefully immerse ourselves day and night in God's Word (Joshua 1:8; Psalm 1:2). Let us also be the sort of Berean-like people who receive good teaching about God's Word "with all eagerness, examining the Scriptures daily to see if these things were so" (Acts 17:11). [7]

5 Questions for personal reflection

*Am I taking time to study and wrestle with the Word?*_____

_____

_____

*Do I regularly ask God for His help to see and understand the Word?*_____

_____

_____

*How often do I take the time to slow down and listen to what the Spirit is saying?*_____

_____

_____

What step can I take to become more like a Berean? _____

_____

_____

6 Take time to pray. Confess ways you may have neglected the study of God's Word. Ask the Lord to help you grow in becoming a student of His Word, someone who eagerly examines the Scriptures daily. Find specific verses from this week's passage to incorporate into your prayer.

_____

_____

_____

_____

_____

7 Continue memorizing verses or passages you have chosen to store in your heart. If you'd like more on the topic of reading the Bible or want help in establishing a habit of Bible reading, here are two suggestions:

When I Don't Desire God, John Piper, chapter 8, pages 115-118

"6 Attitudes We Need When Studying the Bible" on Crossway.org
url: https://www.crossway.org/articles/6-attitudes-we-need-when-studying-the-bible/ *or QR code at right*

O merciful God, incline our hearts to your Word and the wonders of your glory. Wean us from our obsession with trivial things. Open the eyes of our hearts to see each day what the created universe is telling about your glory. Enlighten our minds to see the glory of your Son in the Gospel. We believe that you are the All-glorious One, and that there is none like you. Help our unbelief. Forgive the wandering of our affections and the undue attention we give to lesser things. Have mercy on us for Christ's sake, and fulfill in us your great design to display the glory of your grace.
In Jesus' name we pray, amen.[8]

John Piper

"It is good for me that I was afflicted, that I might learn your statutes."

Psalm 119:71

"I never knew the meaning of God's word, until I came into affliction. I have always found it one of my best schoolmasters."[9]

Martin Luther

Lesson Three

> *The section of verses used for Chapter Three is the longest section used in this study, so it may take longer to complete this chapter. Lesson Three, in particular, might take several days of study to finish. There's no need to rush!*

It would be difficult to study Psalm 119 for very long without acknowledging the acute suffering that the psalmist is enduring as he pours out his anguished heart to his God. It's obvious that he has dealt with suffering in the past and is also dealing with it in the present.

Suffering is a common theme throughout all of Scripture. In this eight chapter study, we will just begin to scratch the surface of what the Word teaches us about suffering. However, from Psalm 119 alone, we can learn a great deal about how we as followers of Christ are to think about and respond to trials and suffering while sojourning on this earth.

Read 119:41-88.

1 Write down a few phrases that clue you in to the author's suffering. Record specific words used to describe his condition:

_____

_____

_____

Jesus tells us in John 16:33, "In the world you will have tribulation. But take heart; I have overcome the world."

Peter, a disciple of Jesus, says this about trials: "Beloved, do not be surprised at the fiery trial when it comes upon you to test you, as though something strange were happening to you" (1 Peter 4:12).

From these passages, as well as countless others, Scripture teaches that suffering is a natural part of this earthly life. James M. Boice, in his *Psalms, Volume 3, an Expositional Commentary*,[10] gives a helpful explanation of the different forms of suffering we might encounter as we live on this earth, waiting for Jesus to return:

> First, some suffering is simply the common lot of man. We live in an imperfect world. We get hurt; we get sick; we die. "Man is born to trouble as surely as sparks fly upward" (Job 5:7).

> Second, there is suffering that is corrective. This is the most obvious category of suffering for most Christians and what is described in Psalm 119:67: "Before I was afflicted I went astray, but now I obey your word."

> Third, some suffering is constructive. That is, it is used by God to sharpen our skills and develop our character: "Suffering produces perseverance; perseverance, character; and character; hope" (Romans 5:3-4).

> Fourth, some suffering is given only to glorify God in it and by it. "It was not that this man sinned, or his parents, but that the works of God might be displayed in Him" (John 9:3).

> Fifth, [some suffering is] cosmic suffering. Cosmic suffering demonstrates before Satan and the angels that a person can love and trust God for who he is in himself and not merely for what he gets out of him. Job is an example of cosmic suffering.

Even while knowing these truths about suffering, I find myself trying to avoid it at all costs. The topic of suffering is an incredibly difficult one. Our finite minds often cannot begin to understand the good purposes in it, the seeming randomness to it, the sheer horror of it. It's safe to assume that most, if not all of us, would never choose suffering if given the option.

And yet, suffering comes. Maybe you are in the midst of suffering, or maybe you are walking closely with someone who is suffering. The author of Psalm 119 is most certainly in the midst of suffering on more than one level. How can he honestly say there are benefits to suffering? And yet he says, "It is good for me that I was afflicted" (Psalm 119:71).

2 Look thoughtfully through verses 65-88.

Which forms of suffering do you think are in view here? _____

_____

_____

What specific benefits do/did the psalmist's afflictions bring him? _____

_____

_____

Record specific actions and attitudes the author chose to have in the midst of his suffering:

Attitudes _____   *Actions* _____

_____   _____

_____   _____

_____   _____

In your own words, how would you describe the psalmist's perspective on suffering in these verses?

_____

_____

_____

_____

3 According to the following passages, what other benefits do we receive from trials?

Romans 5:1-5 _____

_____

Romans 8:16-18 _____

_____

James 1:2-4 _____

_____

4 **Read Isaiah 53:1-12** and record the verbs and phrases used to describe our Savior's suffering:

_____

_____

_____

_____

5 **Read 1 Peter 2:21-23 and 4:12-19** and complete the following:

While suffering, Jesus chose to: _____

_____

_____

While suffering, Jesus chose not to: _____

_____

_____

What phrases from this week's verses in Psalm 119 convey the same perspective as these verses in 1 Peter?

_____

_____

_____

6 This kind of Godward perspective towards suffering requires a diligent "renewing of the mind." (Romans 12:2) Following our Savior's steps and example is not for the faint of heart! Take some time to consider your own personal suffering in light of these truths.

What do you know to be true about God in the midst of your suffering? _____

_____

_____

_____

What specific promises/verses can you trust in / cling to in the midst of your suffering? _____

_____

_____

_____

7 Cry out to the Lord to help you see His goodness in the midst of your suffering. Ask your High Priest, who is well able to sympathize, to pour out His abundant grace that you might have the faith to declare with the psalmist: "You are good and do good" (Psalm 119:68).

If you'd like help in getting started, use the psalmist's requests and compose your own heartfelt prayer:

Let your…

Give me…

May my…

In your…

"Entering the day without a serious meeting with God, over His Word and in prayer, is like … taking a trip without filling the tires with air or the tank with gas. The human heart does not replenish itself with sleep. The body does, but not the heart. The spiritual air leaks from our tires, and the gas is consumed in the day. We replenish our hearts not with sleep, but with the Word of God and prayer. Thousands of saints have discovered through the centuries that starting the day by filling the mind with the Word of God will bring more joy and more love and more power than traveling on yesterday's gas." [11]

John Piper

"If you receive my words and treasure up my commandments within you, making your ear attentive to wisdom and inclining your heart to understanding; yes, if you call out for insight and raise your voice for understanding, if you seek it like silver and search for it as for hidden treasures, then you will understand the fear of the LORD and find the knowledge of God. For the LORD gives wisdom; from his mouth come knowledge and understanding."

Proverbs 2:1-6

"Then the Lord said to me, 'You have seen well, for I am watching over my word to perform it.'"

Jeremiah 1:12

Lesson Four

Read Psalm 119:41-88, noticing many of the words that are used two or more times in this section of verses.

1 Choose at least two of these repeated words and spend time meditating on their meaning and significance. Here are just a few examples of repeated words:

Remember; think of

What does the author remember, rather than forget? What does he ask his God to remember?

Hope

In what does the psalmist place his hope?

Promise

What promises does the psalmist make? What promises does God make?

Comfort

Where does the author find/take comfort? _____

_____

_____

_____

2 Take a second look at the *Teth* stanza, verses 65-72. *Teth* is the first letter of the Hebrew word "good." Notice how many times the word "good" is used in this stanza. Take a minute to jot down the phrases where "good" is used.

_____

_____

In verse 68, the psalmist declares that the Lord *is* good and *does* good. I have never studied Hebrew, but I love to find the original meaning of words in my *Hebrew-Greek Key Word Study Bible*. The Hebrew word used here for "good" is *yatab*, meaning "to do good, right; to make successful, cause to prosper."[12]

Write a sentence or two, explaining how the truth of verse 68 intersects with your present life circumstances.

_____

_____

_____

3 "Delight" is another word used several times in this passage. Where does the psalmist find his delight?

_____

_____

How well can you relate to this? To what degree are you presently finding delight in God's Presence and His Word?

_____

_____

_____

Rather than feeling shame or condemnation, use this opportunity to *cry out* to the One who is eager to help you, to the One who calls you His "chosen ones, holy and beloved" (Col 3:12).

Repent of ways you are delighting in other things or people, more than you are delighting in Him. Our Savior loves to answer these kinds of prayers! He is jealous for our time and affections.

_____

_____

_____

If helpful, use the following prayer and make it your own:

> 66
>
> Merciful Father, help me to "find my delight in your commandments" (Ps 119:47), to love them with all my heart, soul and mind. Please help me to "delight in the way of your testimonies as much as in all riches" (Ps 119:14). Please forgive me for loving and delighting in _____, more than I love and delight in You. By Your Spirit, make me one of the blessed ones, who "delight in the law of the LORD and meditate on it day and night" (Psalm 1:1-2).
>
> 99

5 Spend time hiding your chosen verses/passages in your heart.

"The steadfast love of the LORD never ceases;
his mercies never come to an end;
They are new every morning; great is your faithfulness.
'The Lord is my portion', says my soul, therefore I will hope in him."

Lamentations 3:22-24

"I believe in the power of the indwelling Word of God to solve a thousand problems before they happen, and to heal a thousand wounds after they happen, and to kill a thousand sins in the moment of temptation, and to sweeten a thousand days with the 'drippings of the honeycomb.'"[13]

John Piper

"Let the word of Christ dwell in you richly..."

Colossians 3:16

Lesson Five

Read 119:41-88

1 What declarations does the psalmist make about God and his character in verses 41-88?

God is/God does: _____

_____

_____

Whether in suffering or out of suffering, God's Word is: _____

_____

_____

2 Take a look at verse 84. Do you notice any missing topic that's mentioned in nearly every other verse throughout this psalm?

_____

_____

*Do you think this omission is intentional? Why or why not?*_____

_____

_____

Is it possible that the author is so deeply discouraged that he momentarily forgets the importance of the Word and the promises of the Word?

Spurgeon believes verses 81-88 are the "lowest points" of the psalm: "This octave is the midnight of the psalm, and very dark and black it is. However, even in the blackness, stars....shine out, and the last verse gives promise of the dawn."[14]

*How does the psalmist once again speak truth to himself in verses 86-88?*_____

_____

_____

*What is the "promise of the dawn"?*_____

_____

_____

2 Notice the specific character trait of God that is highlighted at the beginning, middle, and end of this section of Scripture (in verses 41, 64,76, and 88). Go ahead and circle these references.

*According to verse 41, where do we find God's steadfast love demonstrated?*_____

_____

_____

3 Read the entire chapter of **Romans 5 and John 3:16.**

*How does God display His love to all people?*_____

_____

_____

_____

*What numerous gifts do we receive through God's steadfast love?*_____

_____

_____

_____

The entire book of Psalms is replete with the theme of the steadfast love of the Lord! In fact, God's steadfast love is declared 127 different times in the book of Psalms alone. In Psalm 32:10, David makes this declaration: "Many are the sorrows of the wicked, but steadfast love surrounds the one who trusts in the Lord." David clings to the truth that even in the midst of suffering, the Lord's steadfast love will comfort him, sustain him, and give him life!

4 Choose one or more of the following psalms to read: **Psalm 33, 98, or 103.**

Take time to marvel at your heavenly Father and praise Him for loving you with a constant, unconditional, everlasting love! Praise Jesus for dying in your place, the righteous for the unrighteous, and offering you peace and right standing with a holy God. There is *no* greater love than this, that "Someone lay down his life for his friends" (John 15:13).

How precious is your
steadfast love, O God!

...You give [us] drink
from the river of your
delights.

Psalm 36:7a, 8b

5 To complete this lesson and chapter, **read through Psalm 36:5-10,** savoring the beautiful description of our awesome, generous, steadfast, loving God and the benefits available to us when we feast on Him and find our refuge in Him.

Chapter Four

Psalm 119:89-104

"Oh, how I love your law!
It is my meditation all the day."

Psalm 119:97

Steep: *to soak in a liquid at a temperature*
under the boiling point (as for softening,
bleaching, or extracting an essence)
2: to cover with or plunge into a liquid
(as in bathing, rinsing, or soaking)[2]

*"By faith we understand that the universe was
created by the word of God…"*

Hebrews 11:3

*"The Bible is alive, it speaks to me; it has feet, it runs after me; it has
hands, it lays hold of me. The Bible is not antique or modern.
It is eternal."* [1]

Martin Luther

*"On the glorious splendor of your majesty,
and on your wondrous works,
I will meditate."*

Psalm 145:5

Lesson One

Read Psalm 119:89-104

1 Notice the abrupt change of thought and tone as the psalmist begins this stanza. In the previous stanza, verses 81-88, the psalmist is at his lowest point. He is wondering when he will be comforted and groaning over persecution and pitfalls. Now, this worshipper is exclaiming and declaring amazing truths about God and His Word!

Using these verses as your guide, what is the foundation for the psalmist's confidence? Jot down specific phrases that help you come to this conclusion:

_____

_____

_____

_____

It seems that reminding himself of the Lord's steadfast love (verse 88) renews his mind, lifts his gaze upward, and creates spontaneous praise, adoration, and declarations of God's character! He has once again found his footing on the Word.

2 What are the declarations the author makes about God and His Word in verses 89-91? Take time to enjoy these verses—they are filled with meaning!

Declarations: _____

_____

_____

_____

The first declaration the psalmist makes is this: "Forever, O Lord, your Word is firmly fixed…"

Look up the following passages to see similar declarations Scripture makes regarding the eternal Word:

Psalm 138:1-2

What declaration does David make regarding God and His Word? _____

_____

Isaiah 40:6-8

What are the contrasts mentioned here? _____

_____

Matthew 24:35

What is fleeting? What is eternal? _____

_____

One of my favorite college professors used to regularly make this statement, and it has stayed with me for 35 years: "Only two things in this life are eternal—God's living Word and the souls of people. Spend your life investing in these things."

The Word of God lasts forever.

What application does this have for your present life, as well as for your life's purpose and vision?

_____

_____

_____

Matthew 5:17-18

Before reading ahead, put in your own words what you think Jesus is saying here:

_____

_____

_____

Reading this verse in several translations helped me understand the magnitude, power, and awesomeness of Jesus' words. Take a look:

Matthew 5:18 (CEB): "I say to you very seriously that as long as heaven and earth exist, neither the smallest letter nor even the smallest stroke of a pen will be erased from the Law until everything there becomes a reality."

Matthew 5:18 (NRSV): "For truly I tell you, until heaven and earth pass away, not one letter, not one stroke of a letter, will pass from the law until all is accomplished."

66

99

Matthew 5:18 (MSG): "God's Law is more real and lasting than the stars in the sky and the ground at your feet. Long after stars burn out and earth wears out, God's Law will be alive and working."

Matthew 5:18 (KJV): "For verily I say unto you, till heaven and earth pass, one jot or one tittle shall in no wise pass from the law, till all be fulfilled."

We don't use *jot* or *tittle* much these days in our everyday conversation! Here's how Merri-am-Webster defines these terms:

> "***Jot:*** the least bit; iota."

> "***Tittle:*** a point or small sign used as a diacritical mark in writing or printing; a very small part."

3 God's Word is fixed in the heavens for all eternity—because our eternal God keeps His Word.

Read Matthew 24:35

Write it out here: _____

_____

Joshua 23:14

What are Moses' parting words to the Israelites just before he takes his last breath? _____

_____

Isaiah 55:10-11

What are God's promises regarding His Word? _____

_____

4 Although Jesus' name isn't ever mentioned in Psalm 119, His presence permeates verses 119:89-91. Do you see Him?

_____

_____

Look up the following passages and use them to answer these questions:

What truths about our eternal Savior are declared in these passages?

How are these passages similar to or different from what Psalm 119:89-91 tells us regarding the Word?

John 1:1-18 _____

_____

_____

_____

2 Corinthians 1:18-20 _____

_____

_____

_____

Hebrews 1:8-12 _____

_____

_____

_____

Luke 24:44 _____

_____

_____

_____

Jesus' throne is forever and ever, and His years will have no end!

Over 300 references to 61 specific Old Testament prophecies regarding the Messiah were fulfilled in Jesus Christ. God is committed to His Word. No single prophecy concerning His Son will be left unfulfilled. No promise God makes will ever be broken!

5 Let's end our time today in the same vein as the psalmist began in stanza Lamedh— with declaration and adoration! "The One who… inhabits eternity, whose name is Holy" deserves our eternal praise (Isaiah 57:15).

_____

_____

_____

_____

_____

_____

_____

"This Book of the Law shall not depart from your mouth,
but you shall meditate on it day and night, so that you may be
careful to do according to all that is written in it."

Joshua 1:8

"... it is as plain to me as anything that the first thing the child of God has
to do morning by morning is to obtain food for the inner man. Now what is
the food of the inner man? Not prayer, but the word of God; and here again,
not the simple reading of the word of God, so that it only passes through
our minds, just as water runs through a pipe, but considering what we read,
pondering over it, and applying it to our hearts."[4]

George Müller

"… For your testimonies are my meditation …"

Psalm 119:97b

Lesson Two

Read Psalm 119:89-96.

1 Look again at the truths the psalmist declares about the eternal Word. These meditations help him turn from the despair of the previous stanzas to a place of praise and rejoicing.

What are the 3 things the psalmist declares the eternal Word has done for him?

v. 92: ....

....

v.93: ....

....

v. 94, 95: ....

....

The eternal Word has rescued, renewed, and saved him! The understanding the psalmist has gained from the Word does not come from the quick "check the box" kind of reading. In order for these truths to make a difference in his current mental and emotional state, the psalmist has certainly studied, stored up, and meditated on the statutes and promises of His

God previously. It's the Word, with the help of the Spirit, that enables him to alter his thinking and focus on unchanging truths in the midst of changing circumstances. In order for the Word to affect our way of thinking and intersect with our circumstances, we must spend time steeping ourselves in the Word by meditating on it.

> ***Steep:*** to soak in a liquid at a temperature under the boiling point (as for softening, bleaching, or extracting an essence). 2: to cover with or plunge into a liquid (as in bathing, rinsing, or soaking).

66

> The word meditation in Hebrew means to speak or mutter. When this is done in the heart, it is called musing or meditation. So, meditating on the Word of God day and night means to speak to yourself the Word of God day and night and to speak to yourself *about* it- to mull it over, to ask questions about it and answer them from the Scripture itself, to ask yourself how this might apply to you and others and to ponder its implications for life…[5]

99

2 Circle or highlight the many times "meditate" is used in Psalm 119 (v. 15 ,23, 27, 48, 78, 97, 99,148). For what purposes and in what situations does the psalmist use meditation?

Situations for meditation: _____

Purposes or benefits of meditation: _____

Here are just a few of the many additional verses from God's Word that teach us to meditate. Use the chart above to add any additional insights you glean from the following verses:

Joshua 1:8

Psalm 19:14

Psalm 104:34

Psalm 143:5

Meditation in our modern world has many connotations and sometimes refers to an emptying of the mind. Scriptural meditation involves filling, saturating, and steeping our minds in the eternal, inerrant, God breathed Word and then speaking those truths back to ourselves.

> 66 Have you realized that most of your unhappiness in life is due to the fact that you are listening to yourself instead of talking to yourself? Take those thoughts that come to you the moment you wake up in the morning. You have not originated them, but they are talking to you, they bring back the problems of yesterday, etc. Somebody is talking. Who is talking to you? Yourself is talking to you. Now this man's treatment ... was this: instead of allowing this self to talk to him, he starts talking to himself. 'Why art thou cast down, O my soul?' he asks. His soul had been depressing him, crushing him. So he stands up and says, 'Self, listen for a moment, I will speak to you.'[6] 99
>
> *Martyn Lloyd-Jones*

3 Read verses 89-104. Spend some time answering these questions and speaking truth back to yourself:

What are the gifts of God declared in this section?

*How can these gifts make a difference in my thoughts and actions today?*_____

_____

_____

_____

What specific truths in this passage bring help, wisdom, or encouragement to my heart and life today?

_____

_____

_____

Recount and name specific ways the Word has helped you in the past. _____

_____

_____

_____

*How can or does the Word bring perspective to your past?*_____

_____

_____

_____

*What is one specific way you desire/need the Word to help you presently?*_____

_____

_____

_____

4 Take time to fellowship with your God about these things. Praise Him for the gift of His Word and His Son. Repent of ways you have neglected or cheapened His Word. Humbly bring your questions to God. Listen for His loving response.

66 The Bible is the Word of a living Person, Jesus Christ, who is our God and Savior. Therefore, read and meditate and memorize with a view to seeing him in the words that he records and the works he recounts. He is as near as your own breathing and is infinitely merciful and mighty.[7] 99

John Piper

"Our minds are vaults especially designed to stockpile the seeds of God's Word. ...the simple seeds of Scripture are priceless assets in times of drought, doubt and difficulty. We can leave our children no inheritance more valuable than the legacy of God's Word." [8]

Robert J. Morgan

"You have established the earth, and it stands fast.
By your appointment they stand this day, for all things are Your servants."

Psalm 119:90b-91

"Maker, and sov'reign Lord
Of heav'n and earth, and seas!
Thy providence confirms thy Word,
And answers thy decrees." [9]

Isaac Watts

Lesson Three

I am convinced that whole studies could be written on verses 89-91 alone! The implications of the psalmist's declarations about God and His Word in these verses are boundless, urgent, and of great importance.

During Lesson One, we focused on the eternal character of God's Word. Today, we will focus on the sovereignty of God shown in His Word. Understanding God's sovereignty (as best as our finite minds are able) is of the utmost importance. What we believe about God's control—or lack thereof—powerfully shapes how we interpret and respond to everything that happens to us and our loved ones, as well as how we interpret events all around the world.

Here's how *The Westminster Confession of Faith* defines God's sovereignty: "God, from all eternity, did, by the most wise and holy counsel of His own will, freely, and unchangeably ordain whatever comes to pass." Bible teacher and author Arthur W. Pink explains God's sovereignty this way:

> To say that God is sovereign is to declare that God is God. To say that God is sovereign is to declare that He is the Most High, doing according to His will in the army of heaven, and among the inhabitants of the earth, so that none can stay His hand or say unto Him what doest Thou? (Daniel 4:35) To say that God is sovereign is to declare that He is the Almighty, the Possessor of all power in heaven and earth, so that none can defeat His counsels, thwart His purpose, or resist His will. (Psalm 115:3) To say that God is sovereign is to declare that He is The Governor among the nations. (Psalm 22:28), setting up kingdoms, overthrowing empires, and determining the course of dynasties as pleaseth Him best. To say that God is sovereign is to declare that He is the Only Potentate, the King of kings, and Lord of lords. (1 Timothy 6:15) Such is the God of the Bible.[10]

1 The truth of God's absolute sovereignty is a recurring theme throughout both the Old and the New Testaments. Take time to read, make notes, and meditate on two or more of the following passages:

Isaiah 44:24-28

Isaiah 48: 12-13

Daniel 2:20-22; 4:34-35

1 Chronicles 29:10-16

_____

_____

_____

_____

_____

_____

Look again at the psalmist's declarations in verses 90 and 91.

66 ...You have established the earth, and it stands fast. By your appointment they stand this day, for all things are your servants. 99

The author of Psalm 119 is standing firm on the unshakable rock of God's sovereignty and His eternal Word. If God were not a "God merciful and gracious, slow to anger and abounding in steadfast love and faithfulness" (Psalm 86:15), we would have cause to fear His sovereignty. But our God is all of those things! He is completely trustworthy as our Sovereign King.

Just as the author of Psalm 119 declared in verse 68, we can also declare: "In your sovereignty, Lord, 'You are good and do good.'"

Once again, Jesus' sovereign power and presence is strong in this stanza. Can you hear the song of praise the psalmist is singing to Jesus?

2 Use the following passages to answer these questions:

Colossians 1:15-20

Hebrews 1

Who "established the earth and holds it fast"?

What role did Jesus have in creation?

What is Jesus doing now while He waits to return to Earth and bring His children home?

 3 Take some extended time to steep yourself in Psalm 119 and other passages from this chapter. Praise our eternal, sovereign King for His good and loving control. Declare your trust in His sovereign plan for your life—past, present, and future.

4 Continue memorizing your chosen verses/stanzas. Store up His eternal Word.

"Great is thy faithfulness, O God my Father,
There is no shadow of turning with Thee;
Thou changest not,
Thy compassions they fail not;
As Thou hast been Thou forever will be.
Great is Thy faithfulness!
Great is Thy faithfulness!
Morning by morning new mercies I see;
And all I have needed Thy hand hath provided—
Great is Thy faithfulness,
Lord, unto me!" [11]

Thomas O. Chisholm (1923)

"For the word of the Lord is upright,
and all his work is done in faithfulness."

Psalm 33:4

"I pray, O God, that I may know You and love You, so that I may rejoice in You…..May I receive what you promise through Your truth so that my 'joy may be complete'. God of truth, I ask that I may receive so that my 'joy may be complete.' Until then let my mind meditate on it, let my tongue speak of it, let my heart love it, let my mouth preach it. Let my soul hunger for it, let my flesh thirst for it, my whole being desire it, until I enter into the joy of the Lord,' who is God, Three in One, 'blessed forever. Amen'." [12]

St. Anselm
Proslogion, 1077-1078

Lesson Four

1 Read Psalm 119:89-104

I am having trouble moving past verses 89-91!

Verse 90 highlights yet another of God's attributes, His faithfulness.

The psalmist shouts, 'Your faithfulness endures to all generations" (Psalm 119:90).

Having reminded himself of the abundant life found in the steadfast love of the Lord (verse 88), the author is declaring and proclaiming the awesome attributes of His God!

In Psalm 36:5, David proclaims a similar truth: "Your faithfulness, O God, extends to the clouds." The writer of Psalm 89:1 is so confident in God's faithfulness that he wants to declare it to others: "with my mouth I will make known your faithfulness to all generations."

> "The psalmist affirms, over and over, the Lord's certainty and stability."[13]
>
> ***David Powlinson***

Do the roots of God's Word go down deep enough in our souls that we will remain confident in our God even when He chooses to be silent in our present situation? Are we consistently steeping ourselves in the truths of God's character, so that we will have the faith and confidence necessary to stand on His eternal promises, His faithfulness, His sovereignty, even when disappointments and sufferings come? "O, Lord, we believe; help our unbelief" (Mark 9:24).

In order to build our faith, let's spend some time today steeping ourselves in the truth of His faithfulness.

Deuteronomy 32:4

*What words are used here to describe our God?*_____

_____

_____

2 God is faithful to His Word:

Using the passages below, record the many repeated words used to describe how faithful God is to His Word:

Joshua 21:45 _____

_____

Joshua 23:14 _____

_____

1 Kings 8:56 _____

_____

Ezekiel 12:25 _____

_____

Hebrews 6:13-18

What are the two unchangeable things highlighted here? _____

_____

In what specific ways does this passage bring hope and encouragement to you? _____

_____

3 God is faithful to His children:

Deuteronomy 7:6-9

Record the phrases that declare His faithfulness:

Using the following verses, write down some specific and active ways in which God is faithful to you, His child.

1 Corinthians 10:13

1 Thessalonians 5:23-24

2 Thessalonians 3:3

Hebrews 10:23

"Praise befits the upright."

Psalm 33:1b

"The one who offers thanksgiving as his sacrifice glorifies me..."

Psalm 50:23a

"...Sing to the Lord a new song.... Let the godly exult in glory; let them sing for joy on their beds. Let the high praises of God be in their throats..."

Psalm 149:1, 5-6

"Let everything that has breath praise the Lord!"

Psalm 150:6a

4 Let's conclude our time today by steeping ourselves in **Revelation 19:11-16.**

Jesus, our Eternal and Sovereign Savior, is known by hundreds of names in Scripture. Some scholars say Jesus has over 700 different names! What 5 beautiful, powerful names is Jesus called by in this passage?

_____

_____

_____

5 Shout, sing, and worship at the feet of Him who is called "The Word of God"!

_____

_____

_____

_____

_____

_____

_____

_____

*"It is he who made the earth by his power,
who established the world by his wisdom, and
by his understanding stretched out the heavens."*

Jeremiah 10:12

*"Meditation means reading the Bible and chewing on it to get the sweetness
and the nourishment from it that God designs to give. It should involve memorizing the Word so that you can chew on it and be strengthened by it during
day and night…. Think and mull and ponder and chew until you see God
as precious and valuable and beautiful and desirable."* [14]

John Piper

*"If any of you lacks wisdom, let him ask God,
who gives generously to all without reproach, and it will be given him."*

James 1:5

Lesson Five

Read Psalm 119:97-104.

The entire book of psalms regularly employs parallelism, a structure often used in Hebrew poetry. Parallelism simply means that the words of two or more lines of text are directly related in some way.

The psalmist uses parallelism in verses 98-100 to help us understand the first of several reasons why the author loves God's Word and why we should love it too. In these three verses, the psalmist finds three ways to declare that loving and meditating on God's law (the whole counsel of God) brings *wisdom* beyond his years!

1 Search verses 101-104 to see and record several other reasons why the psalmist loves the Word of God:

_____

_____

_____

Who is our Teacher when we study and meditate on the Word? (v. 102b) _____

_____

"All Scripture is breathed out by God and profitable for teaching..."

2 Timothy 3:16

"[Wisdom] is more precious than jewels, and nothing you desire can compare with her."

Proverbs 3:15

Notice the NIV translation for this verse: "… for you *yourself* have taught me" (italics added). We really can't remind ourselves too often of this truth: when we read the Word, God Himself is actually speaking to us! Because of and through the Lord's mercy, grace and kindness, we are students in the classroom of God!

Since we will take extended time in future lessons to highlight many of the other benefits declared here, today we will focus on the high value the Lord places on gaining wisdom.

2 Proverbs chapters 1 through 9 are overflowing with pictures of what wisdom looks like and how we are to "search for it as for hidden treasures" (Proverbs 2:4). If you have the time, steep yourself in these chapters. If your time is limited, look up these specific passages:

Proverbs 2:1-10

*Where does wisdom come from?*_____

_____

*What is our responsibility in gaining wisdom?*_____

_____

*What actions should a person take to gain wisdom?*_____

_____

Proverbs 4:20-27

Our ears, eyes, mouth, feet and hearts have a role in obtaining wisdom. What are the specific things they do to gain wisdom?

*Ears:*_____

_____

*Eyes:*_____

_____

*Mouth:*_____

_____

*Feet:*_____

_____

*Heart:*_____

Proverbs 2:22, 4:10-19

*What is the opposite of wisdom?*_____

Proverbs 2:6-8; 3:5-7

*In what ways are we to be dependent upon the Lord in our pursuit of wisdom?*_____

_____

_____

Proverbs 8:12- 21

*Jot down a few of the many benefits gained by having wisdom.*_____

_____

_____

Using the above passages, write down several characteristics of a wise person:

_____

_____

_____

_____

3 Let's take time and ask the Lord to "search us and know our hearts" (Psalm 139:23).

*In what areas of life am I demonstrating wisdom?*_____

_____

_____

Are there areas where I am practicing folly or wickedness? Take the opportunity to get feedback from some-one who knows you well.

_____

_____

_____

*Do I have specific areas of my life where I am wise in my own eyes?*_____

_____

_____

*How would my husband, sister, or friend say I receive instruction and/or correction?*_____

_____

_____

Can I call to mind times when I have ignored, rejected, justified, or scorned instruction or reproof from the Lord or fellow believers?

_____

_____

Ask your patient and long-suffering Savior, the One who sympathizes with your weaknesses, what practical step or steps He wants you to take in repenting and/or gaining and loving wisdom:

_____

_____

4 Lest we go away in despair, *remember* and *respond to* this spoken Word from our wise Teacher:

> "Whoever conceals his transgressions will not prosper, but he who confesses and forsakes them will obtain mercy."

Proverbs 28:13

> "If we confess our sins, he is faithful and just to forgive us our sins and to cleanse us from all unrighteousness."

1 John 1:9

Ask the Lord for grace to confess, repent, and receive His cleansing mercy and forgiveness.

_____

_____

_____

_____

Then **read Proverbs 8:22-36.**

Ponder, stand in awe, and rejoice in Jesus Christ, who is wisdom in human form!

> "For whoever finds me finds life and obtains favor from the Lord."
>
> *Proverbs 8:35*

> "....to the only wise God be glory forevermore through Jesus Christ! Amen."
>
> *Romans 16:27*

> "Now unto the King eternal, immortal, invisible, the only wise God, be honor and glory for ever and ever. Amen."
>
> *1 Timothy 1:17 KJV*

Chapter Five

Psalm 119:105-128

Your testimonies are my heritage forever, for they are the joy of my heart.

Psalm 119:111

 Savor: *to taste or smell with pleasure; to delight in[1]*

"His delight is in the law of the Lord,
and on his law he meditates day and night."

Psalm 1:2

"Your words were found, and I ate them, and your words became to me a
joy and the delight of my heart, for I am called by your name,
O Lord, God of hosts."

Jeremiah 15:16

"'Son of man, feed your belly with this scroll that I give you
And fill your stomach with it.'
Then I ate it, and it was in my mouth,
As sweet as honey."

Ezekiel 3:3

Lesson One

Read Psalm 119:105-128.

1 In verse 105, the psalmist declares that God's Word is a lamp to his feet and a light to his path. The Hebrew word for "light" that is used in this verse means "to be resplendent with light." Webster's definition of resplendent is "shining brilliantly; characterized by a glowing splendor."

Using these definitions, in a sentence or two, how would you explain the significance of knowing and using God's Word to direct your life's path?

_____

_____

_____

Both the Old and the New Testaments are rich in passages that reference light.

For example …

> "…Even the darkness is not dark to You; the night is bright as the day, for darkness is as light with You." (Psalm 139:12)

> "…God is light, and in Him is no darkness at all." (1 John 1:5)

Read one or more of the following passages and marvel at how God was providing a light and a lamp for His people, even before His Word was ever recorded on paper or scroll.

Exodus 13:17-22

Exodus 14:19-25

Exodus 40:34-38

When we read these passages in Exodus, it's easy to see the miraculous, to sense the Spirit's presence, and to stand in awe of God's holiness. May we learn to have that same perspective, that same holy reverence each time we open our Bibles. This same God of the "pillar of cloud and fire" is speaking to us today, guiding us and providing a path for us to follow as we take one step and then another.

May we give thanks and praise that, just as the pillar of cloud by day and the pillar of fire by night did not depart from before the people, God promises to never leave us or forsake us. Immanuel, God with us, is dwelling in our hearts and minds as we open and respond to His Word.

God's Word brings light to our paths during our days of gladness as well as during our nights of suffering and darkness, according to verse 105.

2 Read through the following passages that show us how God is our Light.

Psalm 27:1

What three descriptions of the Lord God are declared here?

The Lord is my… _____

_____

_____

How do each of these characteristics of God intersect with (make a difference in) your present reality?

The Lord is my light, therefore ... _____

_____

_____

Psalm 36:7-9

Write out verse 9 in your own words: _____

_____

_____

Psalm 104: 1-4

Describe the brilliant garments of our God: _____

_____

_____

3 Consider what it means that Jesus is the Light of the World.

John 1:1-13

Circle or highlight the many references to "light." Take time to meditate on the riches found here.

If you have the time, look up these additional verses in John. How is Jesus described?

John 8:12

_____

_____

John 9:5

_____

_____

John 12:35-36

_____

_____

4 Now read Isaiah 9:1-7 and Matthew 4:12-16. *Exactly* what the prophet Isaiah foretold (down to the apostrophe) was fulfilled in the coming of Jesus our Messiah! We praise you, Lord, that on us "a Light has dawned."

How are you affected by these passages? Write down your mental and emotional responses. _____

_____

_____

Read Psalm 89:15-16

Who are the blessed ones? _____

_____

How do those who walk in His light behave? _____

_____

5 Reflect on the following questions:

Where are you desiring the light of the Word to bring clarity to your day or your night? Be specific.

_____

_____

_____

In what areas of your life, or in the lives of friends or family members, do you need the Light Himself, to dispel the darkness and shine His glory?

_____

_____

_____

If you're in a time of gladness, thank Him and specifically call to mind His many kindnesses.

_____

_____

_____

"Send out Your light and Your truth; let them lead me; let them bring me to Your holy hill and to Your dwelling!"

Psalm 43:3

"'Lift up the light of Your face upon us, O Lord'."

Psalm 4:6b

"For it is You who light my lamp; the Lord my God lightens my darkness."

Psalm 18:28

"For God, who said, 'Let light shine out of darkness,' has shone in our hearts to give the light of the knowledge of the glory of God in the face of Jesus Christ."

2 Corinthians 4:6

If you're in the midst of a time of darkness, find specific verses from Psalm 119 that describe your need for deliverance, wisdom, or guidance.

_____

_____

_____

"Uphold us according to your promises, that we may live."

Psalm 119:116

"Deal with your servant according to your steadfast love."

Psalm 119:124

Put your faith in this promise from the Light of the World:

66 And I will lead the blind in a way that they do not know, in paths that they have not known I will guide them. I will turn the darkness before them into light, the rough places into level ground. These are the things I will do, and I do not forsake them. 99

Isaiah 42:16

6 End your study time by reading **Revelation 21:22-22:5**. Anticipate the day when the glory of God will be your sun by day and your moon at night. Bow in worship at the feet of the Lamb.

_____

_____

_____

_____

_____

"Lead, kindly Light, amid the encircling gloom
Lead thou me on.
The night is dark, and I am far from home,
Lead thou me on.
Keep thou my feet; I do not ask to see
The distant scene; one step enough for me."[2]

John Henry Newman

"Now, I know in my experience that Jesus' light is stronger than the biggest darkness."[3]

Corrie Ten Boom

"I delight to do your will, O my God;
your law is within my heart."

Psalm 40:8

"Your testimonies are my delight;
They are my counselors."

Psalm 119:24

"O Almighty God,
Who pourest out on all who desire it
the spirit of grace and of supplication:
Deliver us, when we draw near to Thee,
from coldness of heart and wanderings of mind,
that with steadfast thoughts and kindled affections
we may worship Thee in spirit and in truth,
through Jesus Christ our Lord.
Amen." [4]

The Book of Common Prayer

Lesson Two

Remember to keep storing up verses in your heart and mind! Spend a few minutes each day committing verses and/or stanzas to memory.

Read Psalm 119:105-128.

In Lesson One, we focused on how the Word is our light, as well as how the Word *brings* light to our path. In verses 106-111, the psalmist lists several ways that the Word's light brings clarity to specific areas of our lives.

The light of the Word brings clarity / godly perspective to my:

◊ Behavior (v.106)

◊ Suffering (v.107)

◊ Worship (v. 108)

◊ Danger and enemies (v.109-110)

And in verse 111, we see that the light of the Word brings clarity to our *heritage*. It's the testimonies of God that point us to the promise and assurance of heaven, which is our ultimate heritage as believers in Jesus.

What specifically, do the testimonies of God tell us about our heritage? Why and how does the psalmist find such joy in this heritage?

1 Let's first take a look at the heritage, or inheritance, that the Lord gave the Israelites, His chosen people. Many Bible translations, including the ESV, often use the word "possession" in place of heritage or inheritance:

> Exodus 6:8 (ESV): "I will bring you into the land that I swore to give to Abraham, to Isaac and to Jacob. I will give it to you for a possession. I am the LORD."

> Exodus 6:8 (NKJV): "And I will bring you into the land which I swore to give to Abraham, Isaac, and Jacob; and I will give it to you as a heritage: I am the LORD."

66

> Leviticus 20:24 (NIV): "But I said to you, 'You will possess their land; I will give it to you as an inheritance, a land flowing with milk and honey.' I am the LORD your God, who has set you apart from the nations."

> Leviticus 20:24 (ESV): "But I have said to you, 'You shall inherit their land, and I will give it to you to possess, a land flowing with milk and honey.' I am the LORD your God, who has separated you from the peoples."

99

Look up Deuteronomy 11:8-12 and Ezekiel 20:1-6.

Then, using all the descriptions from these passages, write a "realtor's description" of this land for a potential buyer!

_____

_____

_____

_____

2 The book of Joshua gives a detailed account of all the lands/territories that the Lord God helped the Israelites conquer and possess. Moses, and then Joshua, completely followed the Lord's instructions in giving specific lands to the 12 specific tribes.

Now let's take a look at the specific *heritage* the Lord gave the Levites, the descendants of Levi and one of the 12 tribes of Israel. Read the Lord's instructions to the tribe of Levi spoken through Moses in Deuteronomy 10:6-9.

How is their inheritance described?

Here are additional references to the unique inheritance of the Levites:

Deuteronomy 18:1-2

Numbers 18:20-24

Joshua 13:32-33 describes yet again the unique inheritance of the tribe of Levi. How would you describe the heritage of the Levites in your own words?

Why does the Lord keep emphasizing the fact that Moses gave the Levites "no inheritance"?

Is God punishing the Levites in some way? At first glance, this inheritance seems rather unfair, until we begin to understand what God is actually saying. The *ESV Study Bible* explains the Levites' inheritance as "The implied blessing of perpetual nearness to the Lord's presence."[5]

Look back at your "realtor's description" of the Israelites' inheritance. The Lord is saying that His nearness is *better* than that!

King David describes his inheritance this way in Psalm 16:5-6: "The LORD is my chosen *portion* and my cup; You hold my lot. The lines have fallen for me in pleasant places; indeed, I have a beautiful *inheritance*" (emphasis added).

The author of Psalm 119 says it like this:

> Verse 57: "The Lord is my portion…"
>
> Verse 111: "Your testimonies are my heritage forever, for they are the joy of my heart."

For the purpose of helping to give us a broader, richer understanding of what the psalmist is declaring, here is verse 111 in several other translations:

> Psalm 119:111 (BBE): "I have taken your unchanging word as an eternal heritage; for it is the joy of my heart."
>
> Psalm 119:111 (NIRV): "Your covenant laws are your gift to me forever. They fill my heart with joy."
>
> Psalm 119:111 (NAS): "I have inherited Your testimonies forever, For they are the joy of my heart."
>
> Psalm 119:111 (NKJV): "Your testimonies I have taken as a heritage forever, For they are the rejoicing of my heart."

3 Look up the following passages to see our *heritage* as sons and daughters of the Living God. What terms and phrases are used to refer to this heritage? (If you have the time, look up these passages in other translations as well.)

Psalm 73:25-26

Lamentations 3:23-25

1 Peter 1:3-5

Take a few minutes to describe, in your own words, our heritage as children of the King. _____

_____

_____

_____

4 Read the following passages and answer this question:

What is the Father and Son's portion or heritage?

Deuteronomy 32:7-9 _____

_____

Psalm 33:12 _____

_____

Talk about a *most unfair exchange!*

5 Answer the following questions as you reflect on Psalm 119:111: "Your testimonies are my heritage forever, for they are the joy of my heart."

Do you really believe that God's Word and His living Presence are better than _____

_____ *(whatever means flowing abundance and lavish gifts to you)?*

Do your everyday thoughts, actions, and priorities confirm this biblical truth—that the Lord's living and active testimonies are better than a life flowing and oozing with gold, silver, and life's richest physical blessings?

_____

_____

How well and often do you take advantage of this opportunity to store up, study, savor, pray through, steep in, surrender to, and sing about this amazing heritage you've been given through absolutely no merit of your own?

_____

_____

We are the Lord's inheritance!

In what specific ways does that motivate you to live a life pleasing to Him? _____

_____

_____

"...give me life, O LORD, according to your word!"

Ps. 119:107b

"I have sworn an oath... to keep your righteous rules."

Ps. 119:106

"...I do not forget your law."

Ps. 119:109

"I incline my heart to perform your statutes forever, to the end."

Ps. 119:112

Plead with Him to give you His true and eternal perspective on the value and preciousness of His active presence in your life.

_____

_____

_____

_____

Tell Him specific ways you desire to live in the good of your inheritance:

_____

_____

_____

_____

6 **Read Ephesians 1:11-14.** Take time to offer personal declarations of praise to Jesus, for securing and keeping for you an inheritance that is imperishable and unfading.

"Accept my freewill offerings of praise, O Lord…"

Ps. 119:108

"Great things He hath taught us, great things He hath done,
And great our rejoicing through Jesus the Son;
But purer, and higher, and greater will be
Our wonder, our transport, when Jesus we see."[6]

Fanny Crosby

"For a day in your courts is better than a thousand elsewhere."

Psalm 84:10a

"How lovely is your dwelling place
O LORD of hosts!
My soul longs, yes, faints
For the courts of the LORD;
My heart and flesh sing for joy
To the living God."

Psalms 84:1-2

"Please, sir, I want some more."[7]

Charles Dickens

Lesson Three

Read Psalm 119:105-128

In C.S. Lewis's book *The Lion, the Witch and the Wardrobe*, a young boy named Edmund finds himself in an enchanted land after entering a dusty wardrobe in the home of his uncle. He quickly encounters the Queen of Narnia, who offers him whatever he would best like to eat. Edmund, without hesitation, requests, "Turkish Delight, please, your Majesty." Immediately, several pounds of Turkish Delight appear, and Edmund begins shoveling it in. "Each piece was sweet and light to the very center and Edmund had never tasted anything more delicious … the more he ate, the more he wanted to eat." Even after finishing all the Turkish Delight, "he still wanted to taste that Turkish Delight again more than he wanted anything else."[8]

The author of Psalm 119 has a similar intense hunger *for* and delight *in* the Word, but here's where the similarities end. Turkish Delight never satisfied Edmund, but God's Word satisfies!

I think of Edmund when I read verses like Psalm 119:127, 119:162, or 42:1-2.

1 If you have the time, **read through all of Psalm 119**, and circle or highlight the many verses that use the word "delight," "love," or "better than."

If time is short, here are a few verses for your consideration:

"Delight": 119:24, 47, 77, 174

"Love": 119:127, 167

"Better than": 119:72, 103

What *brings* the psalmist joy and delight? What *is* the psalmist's joy and delight?_____

_____

_____

_____

There's a famous expression that first came from the medieval writer Geoffrey Chaucer:

"Familiarity breeds contempt."

That phrase that might be sadly true of some things, but certainly not the Word! As Charles Spurgeon said, "Familiarity with the Word of God breeds affection, and affection seeks yet greater familiarity."[9]

As David declares in Psalm 19:8, "The precepts of the Lord are right, rejoicing the heart…" And in verse 10, "More to be desired are they than gold, even much fine gold…"

2 If we aren't at this place of finding our deepest delight in the Word, how do we get there?

Read Jeremiah 15:16 and notice the order of action:

1. _____

2. _____

3. *"Your words became to me a joy and the delight of my heart."*

Read Isaiah 55:1-3. What specific actions does the Lord tell us to take in order to delight in Him?

1. *Come* _____

2. _____

3. _____

3 While studying Psalm 119, I often find myself asking this question: How did the psalmist get to this place where he delighted in God's "testimonies as much as in all riches" (v. 14)? What exactly did he do to cultivate this delight? There's certainly not just one answer to this question, but I'm wondering if looking closely at his numerous requests might not bring us helpful illumination.

Have you noticed how often the author of Psalm 119 shouts out this plea: "Give me life, O Lord, according to Your Word!"? Or how about his heartfelt requests to "incline my heart," "open my eyes," and "unite my heart"?

The psalmist knows without a doubt that he can't possibly muster up delight in his own strength. He can't begin to love the Word more than gold if left to his own devices. He knows the lukewarm state of his heart and affections. He cries out to the One who is eager to "take our hearts of stone and turn them into hearts of flesh" (Ezekiel 36:26).

David makes this appeal to His Lord in Psalm 86:4: "Gladden the soul of Your servant, for to You, O Lord, do I lift up my soul."

Read Ezekiel 36:22-28 and be encouraged that the Father, through Jesus His Son, has already purchased a heart of flesh for us. Take hope in what He continually wants to do in us and is more than able to do, when our hearts feel cold, lukewarm, or unresponsive to His Words of life and delight. Here are some suggestions for how to pray:

Cry out to Him, using specific living and active phrases found in His word.

Thank Him for how He first acted upon your heart through salvation.

Acknowledge your desperate need for His continued help to have a heart that delights in Him more than other things.

There are many painful reasons for a lack of joy/delight in the Word: chronic suffering, tragedy, loss, depression, and unrepentant sin, to name a few. These are real and most certainly not to be discounted. This study is unable to cover the many varied reasons for a lack of joy in the Lord. If you find yourself in this place, *please* don't suffer alone. Share with a pastor, your small group leader, or a wise and trusted friend. Ask others to cry out to God on your behalf!

After you do that, here are a couple of suggestions for your consideration:

66   Lay your dead hearts at Christ's feet, and plead in this manner: Lord, my heart is exceedingly dull and distracted; I feel not those enlarging, melting influences which thy saints have felt; but are they not chief material mercies of the covenant? Doest thou not promise a spirit of illumination, conviction, and humiliation? Is not holiness of heart and life a main branch of it? Dost thou not promise to write thy law in my heart? Now, Lord, these are the mercies my soul wants and waits for. Fill my soul with these animating influences, revive thy work of grace in my soul, draw out my heart towards thee, increase my affection for thee, repair thine image, call forth grace into lively exercise....Remember thy word unto thy servant...O quicken my dull heart according to thy word. [10]   99

Oliver Heywood

66   Resolve to spend most of your time in thanksgiving and praising God. If you cannot do it with the joy that you should yet do it as you can. You have not the power of your comforts: but have you no power of your tongues? Say not, that you are unfit for thanks and praises unless you have a praising heart and were the children of God; for every man, good and bad, is bound to praise God, and to be thankful for all that he hath received, and to do it as well as he can, rather than leave it undone...Doing it as you can is the way to be able to do it better. Thanksgiving stirreth up thankfulness in the heart. [11]   99

Richard Baxter, an English Puritan and theologian

4 Use the following passages to answer this question:

What and whom does God delight in?

Matthew 3:16-17 _____

_____

_____

Jeremiah 9:23-24 _____

_____

_____

Psalm 147:10-11 _____

_____

_____

Psalm 149:4 _____

_____

_____

Zephaniah 3:9-17 _____

_____

_____

"...verse (17) remarkably adds that God himself *will rejoice over you with gladness*, indicating that when God's people seek him and follow him (Zephaniah 3:12-13), and rejoice in him and trust him, (vv. 14-16), then God personally delights in them. This is not an aloof, emotionless contentment, but it bursts forth in joyful divine celebration: *he will exult over you with loud singing.*"[12]

ESV Study Bible

5 Spend time thanking and praising our kind and compassionate Father, Who calls us to *come*, boldly, before His throne of grace. Find amazement in the truth that He delights in and sings over us, not because of anything we have done, but because of the sacrifice of His beloved Son.

"O to grace how great a debtor
Daily I'm constrained to be!
Let Thy goodness, like a fetter,
Bind my wandering heart to Thee.
Prone to wander, Lord, I feel it,
Prone to leave the God I love;
Here's my heart, O take and seal it,
Seal it for Thy courts above."[13]

Robert Robinson, 1757

"Teach me your way, O Lord,
That I may walk in your truth;
Unite my heart to fear your name.
I give thanks to you, O Lord my God, with my whole heart,
And I will glorify your name forever."

Psalm 86:11-12

Lesson Four

1 **Read Psalm 119:105-128** and record the numerous "resolves" the psalmist makes in regard to the Word.

_____

_____

_____

_____

_____

James M. Boice, commenting on these verses, says that walking with God requires great determination, "since there are many contrary paths and much opposition."[14]

The first "contrary path" laid out in these verses is double-mindedness (v. 113). Not only does the psalmist hate this trait in others, his numerous cries for help throughout Psalm 119 indicate that he finds the very same thing in himself. For a few examples, take a look at verses 5, 10, 29, and 36.

2 God's Word gives many warnings about our double-minded tendencies. Use these passages to answer the following questions:

James 1:5-8

James 4:4-10

Revelation 3:14-16

What brings about double-mindedness? _____

_____

What are the characteristics of a double-minded person? _____

_____

What are the antidotes to having a double-minded heart? _____

_____

Is there an area of your life where you find yourself having a wandering, doubting, or double-minded heart?

_____

_____

Ask your Savior for His thoughts on this. Use the passages below, as well as verses from Psalm 119, to make your own personal pleas for His help to give you an undivided heart.

> Teach me your way, O LORD, that I may walk in your truth; *unite my heart* to fear your name.
>
> Ps 86:11, emphasis added

66

99

> The LORD your God will *circumcise your heart* and the heart of your offspring, so that you will love the Lord your God with all your heart and with all your soul, that you may live.
>
> Deuteronomy 30:6, emphasis added

3 Enemies are a frequent and major opposition to the psalmist. (See verses 115, 118, 119, 121, and 122.) Probably only a very few of us can relate to suffering due to enemies. However, all of us do have an enemy who is looking to destroy us. Scripture calls him "the father of lies." Although our God is infinitely more powerful than Satan, we do need to be aware of his wicked schemes. It is only with the Lord's help that we can resist his lies and temptations.

What do you learn about your constant enemy from the following passages?

John 8:44

Matthew 4:1-11

What weapon did Jesus use to fight the devil's wicked schemes? _____

Eph 4:26-27

When do we give Satan a wicked opportunity? _____

Ephesians 6:10-18

How should we fight against him? _____

As disciples of the One who "disarmed the rulers and authorities" of the earth through His death and resurrection (Colossians 2:15), we have no need to fear this enemy.

We do, however, need to be aware of his desire to devour us, so that we can be wise and watchful and well equipped to resist him. James, in chapter 4:7 gives us this promise: When we *submit* ourselves to God and *resist* the devil, he will flee from us.

> "...he who is in you is greater than he who is in the world."
>
> **1 John 4:4b**

4 Questions for reflection:

Where is the "father of lies" tempting you to doubt the character and ability of your faithful, trust-worthy, loving, mighty God? Name those lies. Expose them to the light of God's Word and His Spirit.

_____

_____

_____

_____

_____

What specific steps do you think the Father of your soul desires you to take in order to "take up the whole armor of God"?

_____

_____

_____

_____

_____

Conclude this lesson by reading and praying through **1 Peter 5:6-11**.

Humble yourself before God.

Cast all your cares on the One who cares for you.

Speak truth to yourself about God's character.

Consider finding verses that speak to your doubts/temptations and writing them down to look at through the day.

Thank Him for the hope provided in His promise to "restore, confirm, strengthen, and establish you."

"Two natures beat within my breast; The one is foul, the other blest; The one I love, the one I hate; The one I feed will dominate."

Anonymous

For those wanting more on the topic of the enemy of our souls, I encourage you to listen to "The Fall of Satan and the Victory of Christ," a 2007 sermon from John Piper.

url: www.desiringgod.org/messages/the-fall-of-satan-and-the-victory-of-christ *or QR code at right*

"You are a hiding place for me;
you preserve me from trouble;
you surround me with shouts of deliverance.
Selah"

Psalm 32:7

"For he will hide me in his shelter
In the day of trouble;
he will conceal me under the cover of his tent;
he will lift me high upon a rock."

Psalm 27:5

"God never coerces us. In one mood we wish He would make us do the thing, and in another mood we wish He would leave us alone. Whenever God's will is in the ascendant, all compulsion is gone. When we choose deliberately to obey Him, then He will tax the remotest star and the last grain of sand to assist us with all His almighty power."[15]

Oswald Chambers

Lesson Five

During Lesson Four, we looked at how the "contrary path" of sin, particularly a double-minded heart, and "opposition" from enemies, both physical and spiritual ones, were hindrances to the psalmist's resolves, and *are* hindrances to ours, as well.

1 **Read through Psalm 119:105-128.** Answer this question, using specific verses/phrases from this section to support your answer:

How much confidence and/or hope does the psalmist place in his own resolve and determination?

_____

_____

2 Notice and record the psalmist's many requests for God's help in order to keep his resolves. For example, here's how I would phrase verse 117: "God, I resolve to walk in Your ways continually, but I need You to hold me up."

God, I am placing my hope here: v. 114, 116, 124

I need You to: _____

_____

_____

Once again, we are made aware of the tension in the Christian life, between our responsibility versus what only God can do. In "The Bookends of the Christian Life," Jerry Bridges and Bob Bevington use the term "dependent responsibility"[16] to describe this tension. Notice how the psalmist goes back and forth between declaring his responsibility (his resolves) versus his dependence upon and desperate need for divine help.

3 Look up the following verses to see how this mystery of the Christian life is explained. Keep in mind, however, there will still be some mystery after steeping yourself here! God's ways are much higher than our ways: "For who has known the mind of the Lord, or who has been His counselor?" (Romans 11:34)

2 Corinthians 12:7-10

Colossians 1:29

1 Peter 4:10-11

Philippians 1:6

What is our responsibility in our sanctification?

What gifts does God provide?

Even in his determination to honor the commandments of God, the psalmist is keenly aware that he can't possibly obey even the simplest of commands without the divine help of his God. But the psalmist knows his God. Because he is deeply steeped in the character of his God, he has great confidence in his God! Praise be to our covenant-keeping God that He is *tenaciously committed to our sanctification!*

4 Read the following passages and record the actions/
commitments of God regarding our growth in godliness:

"It is not my ability, but
my response to God's
ability that counts."

Corrie Ten Boom

1 Thessalonians 5:23-24 _____

_____

_____

Ephesians 1:3-6 _____

_____

_____

66 The weakness of our graces, the strength of our temptations, and the
diligence of our spiritual enemies require strong resolutions. We must be
'steadfast and immovable,' and this will make us 'abound in the work of the
Lord.' Let us frame believing, humble resolutions in the strength of God's
grace, with a fear of ourselves, but a confidence in God.[17] 99

Stephen Charnock (1628-1680)

5 The stanza for verses 113-120 has the title Samekh. This, the 15th letter of the
Hebrew alphabet, means "pillar" or "prop." The truth that the Lord is our pillar
is certainly powerfully depicted through the psalmist's declarations and blunt requests
in this stanza.

In verses 114-117, what are the different nouns/verbs used that remind you of a strong pillar or protector?

_____

_____

_____

"The excellence of a shield lies in that it is hard and impenetrable."[18]

**Thomas Manton
(1620-1677)**

Scripture contains hundreds of references that refer to God as our Protector. Here are just a few for your consideration. Use the following verses to complete the sentence.

Psalm 3:3

Psalm 18:2

Psalm 32:6-7

The Lord is my: _____

_____

_____

_____

The author of Psalm 119 also refers to God as his hiding place and shield (v.114). He then requests that this Shield "uphold" him (v. 116).

H. G. Salter, in *The Book of Illustrations* (1840), explains that a true believer's state is like that of a kite soaring in the sky. The kite soars only when the wind blows it and a hand holds the string. The kite has no power whatsoever in itself, to keep it flying in the sky. It is completely dependent upon outside sources. We are like the kite, completely upheld by God's power and hand. Our "whole strength is in God alone"; our entire "security is in the unchangeableness of His nature, and in the efficacy of His grace… In a word, we are 'kept by the power of God, through faith, unto salvation.'"[19]

In verse 117, the psalmist makes a similar request: "Hold me up."

Charles Bridges says this of verse 117:

> Not only the consciousness of my weakness, but the danger of the slippery path before me, reminds me, that the safety of every moment depends upon the upholding power of my faithful God. The ways of temptation are so many and imperceptible—the influence of it so appalling—the entrance into it so deceitful, so spacious, so insensible—and my own weakness and unwatchfulness are so unspeakable—that I can do nothing but go on my way, praying at every step, 'Hold thou me up, and I shall be safe.'[20]

6   Conclude this lesson and chapter by **reading Psalm 91**.

Spend time in fellowship with the Most High.

Ask Him to open your eyes to see His Son Jesus in this psalm.

Thank your Savior that He held fast to His Father in love on our behalf (Psalm 91:14)

Stand in awe that "His faithfulness is [our] shield and buckler" (Psalm 91:4)

Remember and name specific ways the Almighty has:

◊ *"covered you with His pinions" (Psalm 91:4)*

◊ *protected and delivered you from evil*

Worship your Protector and Deliverer for His countless and eternal promises to be your:

◊ *Shield*

◊ *Hiding Place*

◊ *Refuge*

◊ *Fortress*

◊ *Rock*

◊ *Horn of Salvation*

"Now to Him who is able to keep you from stumbling and to present you blameless before the presence of His glory with great joy, to the only God, our Savior, through Jesus Christ our Lord, be glory, majesty, dominion, and authority, before all time and now and forever. Amen."

Jude 24-25

"When I fear my faith will fail,
Christ will hold me fast;
When the tempter would prevail,
He will hold me fast.
I could never keep my hold
Through life's fearful path;
For my love is often cold;
He must hold me fast.
He will hold me fast,
He will hold me fast;
For my Saviour loves me so,
He will hold me fast.[21]"

"He Will Hold Me Fast," Ada Habershon(1906)

Chapter Six

Psalm 119:129-152

"Your testimonies are wonderful;
therefore my soul keeps them."

Psalm 119:11

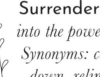

Surrender: *to give oneself up*
into the power of another; yield.
Synonyms: cede, hand over, lay
down, relinquish, turn over[1]

"My son, give me your heart..."

Proverbs 23:26a

"You are not your own,
for you were bought with a price."

1 Corinthians 6:19b-20a

"If thou could'st empty
all thyself of self,
like to a shell dishabited,
Then might He find thee
on the ocean's shelf,
and say "This is not dead,"
And fill thee with Himself instead."[2]

T. E. Brown

Lesson One

Psalm 119 presents a beautiful and powerful picture of a life surrendered to God and His testimonies. Through his "blunt requests, candid assertions, deep struggles, and joyful adorations,"[3] we see a man who continually submits himself to his sovereign Lord.

1 **Read Psalm 119: 129-152** and notice the numerous words or phrases that clue us in to this life of surrender.

When and how does the psalmist yield, or relinquish his rights to His faithful Creator? Keep in mind that you won't find the actual word "surrender," but where do you see attitudes and actions that display a surrendered heart?

Attitudes: _____   *Actions:* _____

_____   _____

_____   _____

_____   _____

2 In Jesus' time of ministry on the earth, He frequently rebuked the Pharisees for their hypocrisy.

> ***Definition of Pharisee:*** a member of a Jewish sect of the intertestamental period noted for strict observance of rites and ceremonies of the written law and for insistence on the validity of their own oral traditions concerning the law.[4]

On the outside, the Pharisees' cups and plates looked very clean (Matthew 23:25), and yet Jesus had very hard and sobering words for them throughout the Gospels. The entire chapter of Matthew 23 is an example: "…you tithe…and have neglected the weightier matters of the law: justice and mercy and faithfulness…you also outwardly appear righteous to others, but within you are full of hypocrisy and lawlessness."

Read the following passages and jot down the phrases Jesus used to describe the actions and attitudes of the Pharisees:

Matthew 15:1-9

Luke 11:37-44

Luke 18:9-14

Antonym of surrender: resist, hold off, usurp.
Near antonyms: battle, contend, defy, object, oppose, repel, thwart, withstand.[5]

The Pharisees did a great job of obeying their man-made laws, but they neglected to follow the greatest commandments: "Love the Lord your God with all your heart, soul, strength and mind, and your neighbor as yourself" (Luke 10:27). Because their "hearts were far from God," they instead focused on the rules they could obey in their own strength—so that they could *appear* righteous while continuing to love themselves and their works more than God.

In contrast, the author of Psalm 119 is focused on loving the Lord his God with all his heart, mind, soul and strength. His desire to obey flows out of a soul surrendered to and devoted to his awesome God. Charles Spurgeon explains the actions and attitudes of the psalmist this way: "His religion was soul work; not with head and hand alone did he keep the testimonies; but his soul, his truest and most real self, held fast to them."[6]

4444444

The psalmist, aware of his tendency to double-mindedness, prays over and over that he may seek and follow God with his whole heart (Psalm 119: 2,10,34,69,145). He is consumed with longing to love and obey God with all that is within him, whether his life as a sojourner is easy or difficult. It seems that he has settled the issue once and for all to trust God, to love God, to follow and obey God, whether he sees God's promises come to pass while still on this earth or not until Heaven. He sings with the songwriter Judson W. Van de Venter, who, in 1896, wrote, "All to Thee my blessed Savior, I surrender all."

3 We will spend the rest of today and tomorrow steeping ourselves in passages that deal with this topic of surrender.

Look up Luke 1:26-38

*Where do you see an attitude of surrender in Mary?*_____

_____

_____

Write out a couple of sentences contrasting the proud, resistant heart of a Pharisee with the humble, surrendered hearts of Mary and the psalmist.

_____

_____

4 Where do you see resistance, contention, or hypocrisy in your own life? Are you aware of an area in your life where you are contending with the Lord, insisting on doing things your own way, or appearing one way but acting another?

_____

_____

_____

Which specific traits of surrender seen in Mary and/or the psalmist do you think God desires to cultivate in you?

_____

_____

Using exact phrases and verses from Psalm 119:129-152, write a prayer to the Lord, declaring your desire to live a life of surrender. Confess specific ways you are living for yourself and/or resisting His plan. Ask for His help to love, obey, and worship Him with your whole heart.

"Accept, O Lord, my entire liberty, my memory, my understanding, and my will. All that I am and have Thou hast given to me; and I give all back to Thee to be disposed of according to Thy good pleasure. Give me only the comfort of Thy presence and the joy of Thy love; with Thee I shall be more than rich and shall desire nothing more."

Suscipe Prayer, Saint Ignatius of Loyola

Father, in this area_____, I confess I am wanting You to do things my way.

I surrender. I lay my desires at your feet and say, "May it be unto me according to your will."

_____

_____

Excerpted from: *"A Prayer for Surrendered Hearts and Straight Paths"* by Scotty Smith[7]

Because of your great love for us in the gospel, we're learning to trust you, not just with our decisions, but also with all the "stuff" in our hearts—our longings, fears, hurts, and dreams. To acknowledge you in all of our ways isn't to *make* you Lord, but to recognize and to rest in your lordship. In fact, we can no more make you Lord of something than we can make water wet, or chocolate good. You are who you are, Hallelujah!

So as we surrender to the occupied throne of heaven, we anticipate straight paths (not necessarily *easy* paths), perfect timing (yours, not ours), and redemptive results (those which reveal your glory and goodness). For those of us dealing with job changes, financial stresses, and health issues, show yourself to be both merciful and mighty, Lord Jesus. May your mercy keep us gentle and your might trump our impatience.

"There is but one way to tranquility of mind and happiness.
Let this therefore be always ready at hand with thee,
both when thou wakest early in the morning,
and when thou goest late to sleep,
to account no external thing thine own,
but commit all these to God."[8]

Epictetus (50-135 AD)

"Love so amazing, so divine,
demands my soul, my life, my all."[9]

Isaac Watts (1707)

"But suddenly what had been an ideal had become a demand—
total surrender to God,
the absolute leap in the dark, the demand was not 'all or nothing,'
that stage had been passed.
Now the demand was simply 'all'!"[10]

C.S. Lewis (1955)

Lesson Two

Jesus Christ is the ultimate example of a life wholly surrendered to His Father.

1 What specific actions or attitudes of surrender do you see in the following passages?

Mark 14:32-42 _____

_____

_____

John 4:34 _____

_____

_____

Hebrews 10:5-7 _____

_____

_____

2 Look up these passages and write out personal application in light of this question:

What type of surrender is the Lord asking of me, His beloved child, today?

Mark 8:31-38 _____

_____

Romans 12:1-2 _____

_____

2 Corinthians 5:14-15 _____

_____

> 66 I have been crucified with Christ. It is no longer I who live,
> but Christ who lives in me. 99
>
> *Galatians 2:20*

3 **Read Psalm 119:129-152.** Look for additional signs of a surrendered heart that you might have missed in your first read-through. Use the chart from Day 1 to record any new insights you find.

_____

_____

_____

_____

4 Read through the songs below and reflect on the words. Share with Jesus why He is worthy of your surrendered heart, mind, and soul.

"All To Jesus I Surrender"
(Israel Houghton, 1896.)

> "All to Jesus I surrender,
> All to Him I freely give;
> I will ever love and trust Him,
> In His presence daily live.
>
> All to Jesus I surrender,
> Make me, Savior, wholly Thine;
> Let me feel the Holy Spirit,
> Truly know that Thou art mine.
>
> All to Jesus I surrender,
> Lord, I give myself to Thee;
> Fill me with Thy love and power,
> Let Thy blessing fall on me.
> *Refrain:*
> I surrender all,
> I surrender all;
> All to Thee, my blessed Savior,
> I surrender all."

"When I Survey the Wondrous Cross"
(Isaac Watts, 1707)

> When I survey the wondrous Cross,
> On which the Prince of Glory died,
> My richest gain I count but loss,
> And pour contempt on all my pride.
> See, from His head, His hands, His feet,
> Sorrow and love flow mingled down;
> Did e'er such love and sorrow meet,
> Or thorns compose, so rich a crown?
> Were the whole realm of nature mine,
> That were an offering far too small;
> Love so amazing, so divine,
> Demands my soul, my life, my all.

5 End your time by singing these songs to the Lord. He loves to hear you sing! Your voice of surrendered worship is pleasing to Him.

"Wonderful are your works;
My soul knows it very well."

Psalm 139:14

"...and his name shall be called
Wonderful Counselor..."

Isaiah 9:6b

Lesson Three

Read Psalm 119:129-144

1 The psalmist makes two declarations in verse 129: "Your testimonies are wonderful; my soul keeps them." For the rest of these two stanzas, he goes on to explain many of the reasons *why* God's testimonies are wonderful.

Record all the reasons you see from these verses. Don't just look for the "right answers"—ask the Lord to open your eyes to see the "wondrous things" in His Word that He wants to reveal to you by His Spirit.

God's testimonies are wonderful because: _____

_____

_____

Wonder: a cause of astonishment or admiration: marvel; miracle; the quality of exciting amazed admiration; rapt attention or astonishment at something awesomely mysterious or new to one's experience.[11]

"Wonder" (and its derivatives, like "wonderful") are used many times throughout the Scriptures. These words occur more than 30 times in the book of Psalms alone! For examples, look back to Psalm 119:18,27.

The author of Psalm 119 makes the bold declaration, "Your testimonies are wonderful," even while he's in the midst of tremendous turmoil and suffering. This is not the response of someone focused on his pain. When we find ourselves in a tumultuous storm, or when

God asks us to walk through a long season of suffering, it is often extremely difficult to see the wonder, the loving goodness, the righteousness, and the faithfulness of our God. God's ways don't always feel wonderful. Our gut-wrenching pain sometimes obscures His wonder and majesty.

How was the psalmist able to testify to God's character in the midst of this suffering? It seems to me that, before the trials came, the psalmist knew his God well and was grounded in the character of his God. By the time "trouble and anguish had found him out," he had settled the truth in his soul that God is righteous, gracious, faithful, good, unchanging, eternal, and steadfastly loving and kind. The psalmist had "well tried" God's promises, and they had all proven true (Psalm 119:140)!

There's no time like the present to get to know our God. What we are able to learn and understand about Him now will greatly influence our ability to trust in His unchanging character when we find ourselves walking through darkness and tremendous pain. God has provided a way to "remain stable and steadfast in our faith, not shifting from the hope of the gospel" (Colossians 1:23). This steadfast faith requires the generous grace of our ever-present Helper, the Holy Spirit.

This requires sitting at the Lord's feet and listening to His teaching. In Luke 10, Martha's sister, Mary, is a wonderful example of the repeated cry in Psalm 119: "Teach me your statutes." In the words of Jesus, "One thing is necessary. Mary has chosen the good portion, which will not be taken away from her" (Luke 10:41). Mary, like the author of Psalm 119, had discovered and delighted in the wonderful teachings of Jesus!

66 Those who know them best
wonder at them most.[12] 99

2 Use the concordance at the back of your Bible to read and savor several other passages that contain these words: wonderful, wonders, and/ or wondrous. Choose one or more of your favorites and write them out here:

_____

_____

_____

_____

_____

_____

Sadly, through the cares of this world, suffering, and/or various other obstacles, we all too often lose this wonder toward God and His Word—or possibly we never had it in the first place. Jen Wilkin believes that for Christian women, "our primary problem is that we lack awe … We can miss majesty when it is right in front of us."[13]

It is October as I write this, and stores are already filled with the sounds and smells of Christmas. I've already spotted Buddy from the movie *Elf* on the store shelves. In the fantasy comedy *Elf*, Santa can't get his sleigh off the ground because there is not enough Christmas spirit in the city of New York.

Allow me to use a silly comparison to ask a serious question. If your sleigh would only fly based on the sense of awe and wonder you have toward God and His Word, would it soar? Or would it sputter to get above the rooftops?

"The law of the Lord is perfect, reviving the soul…"

Psalm 19:7a

If your sleigh is stuck in the snow, what can you do to get it off the ground?

The Word of God has the power and the ability to revive your soul!

"I will praise you with an upright heart, when I learn your righteous rules."

Psalm 119:7
(emphasis added)

Our praise and wonder originates with, and flows out of, our knowledge and understanding of His wonderful testimonies.

3 Our Teacher is inviting us to study His love letter. Use His powerful words of life to cry out to the One who can open our eyes to His wonder and His wonderful testimonies. Meditate on and memorize passages that speak to God's holiness, righteousness, and power.

The passages below might be a great place to begin if you'd like to grow in awe and wonder at our holy, awesome, and righteous God. Choose at least one of these passages to soak in today. Take time to *stop* and *consider* His majesty and His wondrous works.

Exodus 15:1-18

1 Samuel 2:1-10

Psalm 86:8-10

Psalm 99:1-3

Isaiah 40:12-31; 57:15

> Come and see what God has done;
> He is awesome in his deeds toward the children of man.
> Say to God, 'How awesome are your deeds!'
>
> *Psalm 66:3,5*

*"Your righteousness is
righteous forever…"*

Psalm 119:142a

*"Commit your way to the Lord;
Trust in him, and he will act.
He will bring forth your righteousness as the light,
And your justice as the noonday."*

Psalm 37:5-6

*"But seek first the kingdom of God
And his righteousness, and all these things will be added to you."*

Matthew 6:33

"For where your treasure is, there your heart will be also."

Matthew 6:21

Lesson Four

Read Psalm 119:137-144 and highlight the many times "righteous" is used.

"This passage deals with the perfect righteousness of Jehovah and his word, and expresses the struggles of a holy soul in reference to that righteousness."[14] The Hebrew word for "righteous" *(tzedek)* starts with the letter that begins each verse in this 18th stanza of Psalm 119 *(tsadhe)*. One of the many reasons the testimonies of the Lord are wonderful is because in them and through them we see the righteousness of God on display.

Jerry Bridges, a lover of God's holy Word and a prolific author, wrote a great deal on the topic of God's righteousness. He states, "The word righteous in the Bible basically means perfect obedience."[15] He also comments, "As an attribute of God, the righteousness of God refers to who God is in his holiness and perfect justice, and it ultimately means God's unswerving commitment to display his glory and uphold his name."[16]

In Lesson One, we spent some time discussing the righteousness of God, but let's dig a little deeper into this topic.

1 What do you see/learn about the righteousness of God and His Word from this stanza (137–144), as well as from other verses in Psalm 119 (such as 7, 40, 75, 160, 164)?

The righteousness of God: _____

_____

The righteousness of His Word: _____

_____

The psalmist is declaring, shouting from the rooftops, "My God is righteous. His Word is righteous, and all he does is righteous!" Trouble and anguish are very real and near to the psalmist, and yet he knows that God's ways are righteous.

The psalmist *could* be expending his energy doubting the character of God with questions like this: "Are You good? *Will* You be good to me?" Instead, he uses his energy to declare and boast in God: "Righteous you are, O Lord, and right are your ways" (v. 137). Even if his circumstances seem unfair, unjust, and more than he can handle, his mind and his heart are settled on the character of His faithful God. "You are good, and you do good," he declares (v. 68). Later he exclaims, "Righteous are you, O Lord, and right are your rules. You have appointed your testimonies in righteousness and in all faithfulness" (vs. 137–138).

Charles Spurgeon says this of verse 137: "This is a great stay to the soul in time of trouble. It should be our glory to sing this brave confession when all things around us appear to suggest the contrary. This is the richest adoration—this which rises from the lips of faith when carnal reason mutters about undue severity, and the like."[17] Have you noticed just how often the living and active Scriptures highlight God's righteousness *and* His faithfulness in the same breath?

Look up the following verses and record the phrases that speak of these two traits:

Psalm 89:14 _____

_____

_____

Psalm 119:75 _____

_____

_____

Psalm 143:1 _____

_____

_____

Revelation 19:11 _____

_____

_____

How does this truth, that God and His Word are always and forever both completely righteous and utterly faithful, intersect with your reality today? How do these truths about God have the ability and power to change the way you are thinking/worrying about something in the future?

_____

_____

3 Look up Romans 1:16-17

Where is the righteousness of God most clearly revealed? _____

Read 1 Corinthians 15:1-4

In simple words, what is the gospel? _____

_____

66 The good news of the gospel is that Jesus lived a life of perfect righteousness, of perfect obedience to God, not for His own well being but for His people. He has done for me what I couldn't possibly do for myself. But not only has He lived that life of perfect obedience, He offered Himself as a perfect sacrifice to satisfy the justice and the righteousness of God. 99

R.C. Sproul[18]

Read 2 Corinthians 5:21

What is the radical and amazing exchange explained in this verse? _____

_____

I refer again to the winsome and truth-saturated book, *The Bookends of the Christian Life*, in which Jerry Bridges and Bob Bevington present the compelling argument that "the perfect righteousness of Christ, which is credited to us, is the first bookend of the Christian life."[19] As followers of Christ, if we think of each of our lives as a long bookshelf, our unity with Christ and His righteousness must be not only our starting place, but the Truth that holds everything else together. Here are two of my favorite lines from their book (emphasis mine):

> "The news of this righteousness is the gospel.... we're clothed with His righteousness so that as God looks at us in union with Christ, He always sees us to be as righteous as Christ Himself. And that changes everything."[20]

> "We must learn to live like the apostle Paul, looking *every day* outside ourselves to Christ and seeing ourselves standing before God clothed in His perfect righteousness. *Every day* we must *re-acknowledge* the fact that there's nothing we can do to make ourselves either more acceptable to God or less acceptable."[21]

4 Look once again at Psalm 119:137–144. Notice and record particular ways that the psalmist looks *outside* of his feelings and circumstances *toward* God and His faithful ways. In what particular ways do you see the psalmist placing his confidence in Christ's righteousness rather than his circumstances or his own good or bad behavior?

Spend some time rejoicing and exulting in your righteous and faithful God!

"I will greatly rejoice in the Lord;
My soul shall exult in my God,
For he has clothed me with the
garments of salvation;
He has covered me with the
robe of righteousness..."

Isaiah 61:10

"If you prepare your heart,
you will stretch out your hands toward him.

Job 11:13 (ESV)

"If you direct your heart rightly,
you will stretch out your hands toward him."

Job 11:13 (NRS)

"So, commit yourself to God completely.
Reach out your hands to him for help."

Job 11:13 (NIRV)

"...Your name and remembrance are the desire of our soul.
My soul yearns for you in the night;
my spirit within me earnestly seeks you..."

Isaiah 26:8-9a

"Prayer without the heart is but as sounding brass or a tinkling cymbal.
Prayer is only lovely and weighty, as the heart is in it, and no otherwise.
God hears no more than the heart speaks. If the heart be dumb, God will
certainly be deaf. No prayer takes with God, but that which is the travail
of the heart."[22]

Thomas Brooks

Lesson Five

Read Psalm 119:145-152

This final stanza of Lesson Six paints a vivid picture of a surrendered heart praying in the midst of trouble. Those with evil intent are close at hand (v. 150), and yet the psalmist reminds himself and declares that His God is also near and His promises are true (v. 151)! His entire body, mind, and soul appear to be engaged in fervently crying out for help.

1 Use this stanza, as well as what you've observed in past stanzas, to contemplate the following questions:

How does a surrendered heart pray?

What does a surrendered heart ask?

When does a surrendered heart pray?

Where does a surrendered, praying heart place its hope and trust?

Throughout Psalm 119, we see a desperate, humble man continually offering up earnest, raw, and fervent prayers. James 5:16 tells us, "The prayer of a righteous person has great power as it is working." The King James version says it like this: "The effectual fervent prayer of a righteous man availeth much." A righteous person prays fervent, earnest, and effective prayers *with* his whole heart *from* his whole heart!

2 Read James 5:13-18.

*What else do you see/learn about prayer from this passage?*_____

_____

*How is Elijah described in James 5:17–18?*_____

_____

3 To get an in-depth look at Elijah, **read 1 Kings 16:29 through chapter 19**. If you are short on time, focus on chapter 18.

In 1 Kings 17 and 18, not only do miraculous things *happen* to Elijah, the Lord allows Elijah the privilege of participating with Him in order to *bring about* the miraculous. Through the Lord's power, Elijah experienced tremendous success and victory. Why, then, does Elijah so quickly find himself running for his life and hiding in a cave?

How comforting to see that even Elijah, the mighty prophet of God, had a nature just like ours. He was full of faith one day, and cowering in fear and despair the next. How encouraging to learn that God does not require perfection from His children in order for our prayers to be heard. Because of the perfect obedience of His Son Jesus, our gracious Heavenly Father hears our prayers and uses our prayers for our sanctification and for the good of others. How faith-building to know that, as righteous people covered in our Savior's robe of righteousness, our prayers can have the same power as the prayers of Elijah!

4 What words or phrases would you use to describe the prayers of Elijah, a righteous man with a nature like ours?

I am struck by Elijah's patience, perseverance, and tenacity as he prays. Elijah's servant didn't even see a tiny cloud until the seventh trip up the mountain, yet all the while, Elijah is praying, "bowed down on the earth." I find myself asking, "Would I have given up praying after the second trip? Fifth? How often am I willing to stay on bended knee for extended times of prayer?"

5 Look up the passages below to see how the Lord encourages/asks us to persevere in prayer.

Isaiah 62:6-7

Luke 11:5-10 or 18:1-8

The author of Psalm 119 is also certainly an example of a man who persevered in prayer! From today's verses alone (145–152), we see a man who:

- prays earnestly (v.145),
- day and night (v.147–148),
- with faith (v.147),
- while declaring and pleading the promises (v.149).

The psalmist didn't have the same advantage that we do, having God's Word at our fingertips. Yet he had the testimonies "stored up" and ready for use, day or night!

"In all circumstances take up the shield of faith ... and take the sword of the Spirit, which is the word of God, praying at all times in the Spirit, with all prayer and supplication..."

Ephesians 6:16-18

6 Let's conclude this lesson by praying with our Bibles open! Using specific verses from this week's lesson (Psalm 119:129–152), spend some time in surrendered, earnest prayer—praising, thanking, repenting, declaring, and pleading the promises of our mighty God.

"When thou prayest, rather let thy heart be without words than Thy words without heart."[23]
John Bunyan

God Loves to Be Asked

"Now think about this for a moment. God's will is that we, his creatures, ask him for things. And it is not just his will, it is his delight. He loves to be asked for things. Proverbs 15:8 says, "The prayer of the upright is his delight." He is so eager to hear prayers and respond to them that he says in Isaiah 65:24, "It will also come to pass that before they call, I will answer; and while they are still speaking, I will hear." In fact, he takes special steps to see to it that he is constantly badgered. I say that reverently and, I think, truly on the basis of Isaiah 62:6–7, "On your walls, O Jerusalem, I have appointed watchmen; all day and all night they will never keep silent. You who remind the LORD, take no rest for yourselves; and give him no rest until he establishes and makes Jerusalem a praise in the earth." So God loves being asked for things so much that he appoints people to "give him no rest" but to "remind the Lord" and "never [to] keep silent."

(excerpted from John Piper's sermon "Devote Yourselves to Prayer" from January 9, 2000, published on Desiring God.)

Chapter Seven

Psalm 119:153-176

My tongue will sing of Your Word,
For all Your commandments are right.

Psalm 119:11

Sing: *to produce musical tones by means of the voice;*
to utter words in musical tones and with musical
inflections and modulations;
to relate or celebrate something in verse;
to compose poetry;
to make a cry: CALL;
to give information or evidence.[1]

"[Jesus] came that they may have life
And have it abundantly."

John 10:10

"Holding fast to the word of life..."

Philippians 2:16a

"You make known to me the path of life;
In your presence there is fullness of joy;
At your right hand are pleasures forevermore."

Psalm 16:11

Lesson One

Read Psalm 119:153-160.

1 Throughout today's reading, circle each time the psalmist cries, "Give me life …"

Three times in this stanza, the psalmist utters this heart cry: "Give me life"!

Where does the psalmist believe and declare that life comes from? Using the three verses from this stanza, complete the following phrase:

Give me life according to … _____

_____

_____

_____

_____

Now, start back at the beginning of Psalm 119 and highlight the numerous times the psalmist makes a similar plea for life. Use the space above to add any additional phrases you find.

Look at verses 25, 37, 50, 77, 88, 93, 107, 116, 144, 149. What exactly is the psalmist desiring with this request to "give me life"? Do you think he is asking for continued physical life, spiritual life, or both?

I encourage you to use a website such as biblestudytools.com to see how different versions of the Bible translate the phrase, "give me life".

Here's what I found:

KJV - "Quicken me"

NAS - "Revive me"

NIV - "Preserve my life"

NLT - "Renew me"

ESV - "Give me life"

"The Lord has promised, prepared, and provided this blessing of renewed life for all His waiting servants; it is a covenant blessing, and it is as obtainable as it is needful."[2]

Charles Spurgeon

According to the *NIV Hebrew-Greek Key Word Study Bible*, the same Hebrew word, *hayah*, is used throughout this psalm when referring to life. *Hayah* means "To live, recover, revive; to keep alive, preserve a life, save a life, spare a life, restore a life."

2 Let's take a look at various other Bible passages that speak of this life available to all who believe and draw near to God through His Son, Jesus Christ. Where did the psalmist first learn of this provided and prepared life? What promises of renewed life might the psalmist be remembering?

Circle or highlight the various times "life" or "live" is mentioned in these passages. From each passage, write down at least one takeaway regarding this life.

Deuteronomy 30:15-20

Deuteronomy 32:44-47

Psalm 36:9

Job 33:4

Using all that you've gleaned from these passages, write a short paragraph explaining what you think the psalmist is desiring from God with his numerous pleas to "give me life." What is he asking God to do for him? Write as though you are explaining this to someone who is desperate to know the meaning of life and where this life is found!

"The Spirit of God has made me, and the breath of the Almighty gives me life."

Job 33:4

"... in the presence of God, Who gives life to the dead and calls into existence the things that do not exist."

Romans 4:17

"It is the Spirit who gives life; the flesh is no help at all. The words that I have spoken to you are spirit and life."

John 6:63 (emphasis added)

"We must remember that the Word and the Spirit always go together. God speaks to us through both of them working together, and it is also through the Word and not apart from it that the Spirit renews us inwardly."[3]

James Montgomery Boice

"You have been born again [...] through the living and abiding word of God."

1 Peter 1:23

3 As followers of Jesus living on this side of the cross, we have the gift of the New Testament at our fingertips *and* the indwelling Spirit to help us understand God's gift of life. Use the following passages to answer the question:

Where does this life come from, and how do we obtain it?

John 1:1-4 _____

_____

_____

John 6:36,47-51,57-58 _____

_____

_____

John 11:25-27 _____

_____

_____

Romans 4:17 _____

_____

_____

1 John 5:11-12 _____

_____

_____

_____

Hadn't the psalmist already received life? Haven't we as believers in Jesus already received this gift of life? Why do we need to keep asking for it?

In Ephesians 5:18, we are commanded to "be filled with the Spirit." According to John Piper, "...the present tense of the verb in Greek means just that: 'Keep on being filled with the Spirit.'"[4] Scripture tells us that we receive the Spirit when we first receive salvation, but we are also instructed to "keep on being filled with the Spirit." We need to ask our gracious God to do this for us—we cannot "keep on being filled" without His divine help.

In a similar way, we unequivocally receive eternal life when we believe in and surrender to our Savior, Jesus Christ. And yet, without God's regular intervention, our affections will grow cold. We are often double-minded. Amidst distraction by the cares of this world, the "father of lies," and our own weak and sinful flesh, we are all too often tempted to find temporary life, satisfaction, or happiness in things other than our Savior. It's only with the divine intervention of the Spirit, through the power of the Word, that our hearts can be renewed and quickened. Only through the Spirit's work can our souls stay revived and hungry toward God, His Word, and His ways.

4 Praise and thank God for saving you, for making you a new creation and writing your name in "the book of life" (Revelation 20:12)!

Cry out to your faithful God with your own personal pleas for continued life.

Where, specifically, do you need the help of the Spirit to keep renewing your mind, reviving your weary soul, and quickening your spirit to have life according to His Word, His promises, and His mercy?

“
The Spirit and the Bride say, 'Come.'
And let the one who hears say, 'Come.'
And let the one who is thirsty come;
let the one who desires take the water of life without price.
”

Revelation 22:17

“
And this is the testimony, that God gave us eternal life, and this life is in his Son. Whoever has the Son has life; whoever does not have the Son of God does not have life.
”

1 John 5:11-12

"We are his people, and the sheep of his pasture."

Psalm 100:3b

"For the Son of Man came to seek and to save the lost."

Luke 19:10

"I am the good Shepherd.
The good Shepherd lays down his life for the sheep."

John 10:11

Lesson Two

Read Psalm 119:161-176

1 Take some time to compare and contrast these last two stanzas of Psalm 119.

Choose several of the following questions to answer. There are no right answers; they are simply here to help you study and engage with the text.

What title or theme would you give each stanza?
_____
_____
_____

What similarities and differences do you see between verses 161-168 and 169-176?
_____
_____
_____

What similarities and differences do you see between these stanzas and the rest of Psalm 119?
_____
_____

How would you describe the thoughts and emotions of the psalmist in these last two stanzas?

_____

_____

Do you see the psalmist making more requests or declarations in each stanza? _____

_____

_____

What are several of the psalmist's personal resolves/commitments in each stanza? _____

_____

_____

2 From verses 161-176, record the many declarations the psalmist makes towards God and His Word. (Look for words like "You are," "You say," or "You do.")

_____

_____

_____

What does the psalmist ask of God? What are his longings, his pleas?

"I need You to" … _____

_____

_____

3 In verse 170, the author pleads with God to "deliver me according to your word."

How would you explain or describe the kind of deliverance he is longing for? In what specific ways does God's Word bring deliverance?

_____

_____

In verse 174, the longing expressed is for the Lord's salvation. I found Charles Spurgeon's explanation of this verse helpful:

> He knew God's salvation, and yet he longed for it; that is to say, he had experienced a share of it, and he was therefore led to expect something yet higher and more complete. There is a salvation yet to come, when we shall be clean delivered from the body of this death, set free from all the turmoil and trouble of this mortal life, raised above the temptations and assaults of Satan, and brought near unto our God ... Though we have not yet reached the fulness of our salvation, yet we find in God's Word so much concerning a present salvation that we are even now delighted.[6]

4 In the second-to-last stanza, *Sin and Shin*, the psalmist expresses determination and commitment to obey the Lord, praise Him, love righteousness, and hate evil. In the final stanza, *Taw*, he seems to have lost much of his confidence. After nearly 175 verses of proclaiming the attributes of his Lord, remembering the promises of the living Word, and resolving to keep the commandments with his whole heart, he begins the last verse with this surprising thought: "I have gone astray..."

It has taken some time for me to understand why the psalmist ends this magnificent psalm—described as "a touch-stone for the spiritual life of those who read it"[7]—in this manner. It seems that all of his remembering and declaring, and all his many hymns of praise, have only served to make him even more aware of his frailties, his sin, and his inability to do anything good apart from divine power. Paul comes to a similar conclusion in the book of Romans.

Read Romans 7:14-25. What facts does Paul declare to be true about himself from this passage?

_____

_____

_____

Several godly commentators who have studied Psalm 119 through the years believe the psalmist ends with the only appropriate response. Apart from God's deliverance and salvation, he is a lost sheep, going astray at every turn.

"... there is never a moment, even after we are saved, when we can stop thinking of ourselves as lost sheep."[8]

James Montgomery Boice

Read Luke 18:9-14. The tax collector certainly thought of himself as a wandering sheep in need of grace in the parable found in Luke.

Describe the tax collector's opinion of himself. What is his plea?

_____

_____

_____

The songwriter Robert Robinson understood what it means to be a "lost sheep" when he wrote, "Prone to wander, Lord, I feel it, Prone to leave the God I love," in the hymn "Come, Thou Fount of Every Blessing."

Jesus Himself declares this about his sheep in John 15:5: "Apart from Me you can do nothing."

Barton Bouchier believes this verse gives such "an insight into our poor wayward hearts"...(we are) "not merely liable to wander, but ever wandering, ever losing our way, ever stumbling on the dark mountains, even while cleaving to God's commandments!"[9]

66

All we like sheep have gone astray,
we have turned—every one—to his own way;
And the Lord has laid on Him the iniquity of us all.

99

Isaiah 53:6

Our "great Shepherd of the sheep"(Hebrews 13:20) has taken all of our wayward, sinful thoughts and deeds upon Himself and paid the ultimate price for those sins with His own spotless blood. Here lies the hope for all of us!

5 Study the following passages and respond to the questions below.

Psalm 23

John 10:1-18

What actions does our faithful Shepherd take in these passages?

_____

_____

What are the traits and responses of His sheep?

_____

_____

What are the benefits for sheep in His fold?

_____

66

He will tend His flock like a shepherd;
He will gather the lambs in His arms;
He will carry them in His bosom,
And gently lead those that are with young.

99

Isaiah 40:11

Take time to:

Praise Him for taking all of your iniquities upon Himself and paying the price once and for all.

_____

_____

66 Now to Him who is able to keep you from stumbling and to present you blameless before the presence of His glory with great joy, to the only God, our Savior, through Jesus Christ our Lord, be glory, majesty, dominion and authority, before all time and now and forever. 99

Jude 24-25

Thank Him for specific traits of His Shepherding that have recently ministered to you.

_____

_____

66 I am the good shepherd. 99

John 10:14a

Confess ways you have recently wandered from the fold or deliberately gone your own way.

_____

_____

66 He Himself bore our sins in His body on the tree,
that we might die to sin and live to righteousness.
By his wounds you have been healed.
For you were straying like sheep,
but have now returned to the Shepherd and Overseer of your souls. 99

1 Peter 2:24-25

> Yet let the reader remember the first verse of the psalm while he reads the last; the major blessedness lies not in being restored from wandering, but in being upheld in a blameless way even to the end.[10]

Charles Spurgeon

> The strength to follow Your commands could never come from me
> O Father, use my ransomed life in any way You choose
> *And let my song forever be, My only boast is You*

Jordan Kauflin, "All I Have is Christ" (emphasis mine)

"Oh, sing to the LORD a new song;
Sing to the LORD, all the earth!
Sing to the LORD, bless his name;
Tell of his salvation from day to day."

Psalm 96:1-2

"Sing lustily and with a good courage.
Beware of singing as if you were half dead, or half asleep;
But lift up your voice with strength.
Be no more afraid of your voice now, nor more ashamed of its being heard,
than when you sung the songs of Satan."

From John Wesley's preface to "Sacred Melody," 1765

"My heart overflows with a pleasing theme;
I address my verses to the king;
my tongue is like the pen of a ready scribe."

Psalm 45:1

Lesson Three

Read Psalm 119: 161-176

1 As mentioned in the introduction to this study, the title "Psalms" comes from *psalmois*, which means "songs for the accompaniment of a stringed instrument."[11] The Psalms have been called "the hymnbook of the Old Testament."

Psalm 119 is a long song that crosses into a plethora of genres! I find myself wondering if each stanza was sung to the same tune or if each one had a different melody. How do you imagine these verses sung?

_____

_____

I have to think some stanzas were sung slowly, like a dirge, while others had a fast and desperate beat. I can hear verses 89-91 sung boldly, jubilantly, with a full orchestra accompaniment! Maybe the song in verses 25-32 was a precursor to the Beatles mantra "Help, I Need somebody, Help!"[12]

If the living and active God-breathed Word contains a songbook smack dab in the middle of its pages, God must consider the practice of singing pretty significant in the everyday life of a believer!

Two times in Psalm 119, we see the actual word "sing" or "song." If we employ Webster's definition of sing, which includes "cry, call, give evidence," there are dozens of words throughout this psalm that can refer to singing.

The first time we encounter the actual word "song" is in verse 54:

> "Your statutes have been my songs in the house of my sojourning."

Here's how this verse reads in several other translations:

> Psalm 119:54 (BBE) "Your rules have been melodies to me, while I have been living in strange lands."

> Psalm 119:54 (CSB) "Your statutes are [the theme of] my song during my earthly life."

> Psalm 119:54 (GNT) "During my brief earthly life I compose songs about your commands."

> Psalm 119:54 (NRS) "Your statutes have been my songs wherever I make my home."

> Psalm 119:54 (MSG) "I set your instructions to music and sing them as I walk this pilgrim way."

> Psalm 119:54 (NIV) "Your decrees are the theme of my song wherever I lodge."

"Travelers sing to deceive the tediousness of the way. Great is the comfort that cometh in by singing of Psalms with grace in our hearts."[13]

John Trapp

"Such songs have power to quiet
The restless pulse of care,
And come like the benediction
That follows after prayer."[14]

Henry Wadsworth Longfellow (1807-1882)

Write out your favorite translation of this verse here:

Notice the verses surrounding verse 54. How would you describe the circumstances surrounding the psalmist's songs?

2 The second time "sing" is used in Psalm 119 is found in our text for this lesson:

"My tongue will sing of your word, for all your commandments are right" (v. 172).

What thoughts and emotions do you see the psalmist expressing during this stanza, verses 169-176?

_____

_____

3 In his book *How to Read the Psalms*, Tremper Longman III divides the psalms, or poetic songs, into 7 different genres. I found his explanations and examples very helpful:

"The Hymn" begins "with a call to worship" and includes specific reasons for "exuberant praise"[16] of the Lord. For example, Psalm 92 is a hymn.

Read Psalm 92 *and record several of the reasons the psalmist gives for expressing exuberant praise.*

_____

_____

Where do you see examples of a possible hymn in verses 119:161-176? Write down specific reasons the psalmist gives for expressing this exuberant praise:

_____

_____

"The Lament" (such as Psalm 85) "is the psalmist's cry when in great distress he has nowhere to turn but to God."[17] Although "a lament predominantly reflects a downcast mood…all laments include some expression of trust in God", and "hymns of praise are common toward the conclusion of a lament. As the psalmist realizes what God can and will do for him, it leads him to praise God." As we've previously discussed, Psalm 119 contains numerous songs of lament.

Read Psalm 85. *From what you read here, as well as from what you've seen in Psalm 119, record a few of your observations about songs of lament:*

_____

_____

_____

"Thanksgiving Psalms" are another category: "The thanksgiving psalm is a response to answered lament. (It) is praise to God for answered prayer."[18] Psalm 18 is an example of this.

In *"Psalms of Confidence,"* "the psalmist asserts his trust in God, though enemies or some other threat are present."[19] Psalm 119 certainly contains numerous examples of this!

Find a few of your favorites from Psalm 119 and write them here. In what does the psalmist place his confidence? How does he go about singing of this confidence?

_____

_____

_____

"Psalms of Remembrance" are those psalms "in which God's past and acts of redemption are the focus of attention."[20]

Read Psalm 106:1-12 *to see an example of this. Which of God's mighty acts are remembered here?*

_____

_____

_____

"*Kingship Psalms*" [21] include a focus on either the "human king of Israel" (Psalm 20) or "God as King" (Psalm 47:7).

The entire chapter of Psalm 119 is considered the best-known example of a "*Wisdom Psalm*".[22] Wisdom psalms "reveal God's will in the nitty-gritty and difficult areas of our lives." They "emphasize a contrast in ways of living."

Look at verses 155-160 and record the contrast in actions and desires between the godly and the ungodly (wicked, faithless). Find one or more additional examples of either a "contrast in ways of living" or "God's will in the... difficult" from this psalm.

_____

_____

_____

4 What circumstances do you find yourself in as you complete this lesson? Are you presently more inclined to sing a song of confidence or a song of lament, a hymn of praise or a song of remembrance?

Which of the seven genres are you needing to sing today in order to speak truth to yourself?

Think of a song you know that best explains what's on your heart. Sing it to the Lord.

Either use the written Word or offer a verbal prayer (song) to the One who gives us so many reasons to sing.

If you find yourself focused on and worried about a situation in your life, pray and sing a psalm of *remembrance*. End with a song of *thanksgiving*. Recall and name specific ways God has intervened in your past to bring deliverance and/or show His faithfulness.

Maybe you are in the midst of painful suffering. Use a song of *lament* like Psalm 22, 42, or 43. Humbly ask your own questions of the Lord. Express your grief and fears. Declare your trust and *confidence* in a specific attribute of God's.

I find it thought-provoking that, no matter the genre of song, most songs in the Word end by praising and thanking the Giver of life!

"Praise befits the upright."

Psalm 33:1

"It is good to give thanks to the Lord,
To sing praises to your name, O Most High;
To declare your steadfast love in the morning,
And your faithfulness by night,
To the music of the lute and the harp,
To the melody of the lyre."

Psalm 92:1-3

"Those who know Him best sing the loudest!"[23]

Mike Bullmore, pastor

"I sing the goodness of the Lord,
who filled the earth with food,
Who formed the creatures through the Word,
and then pronounced them good."

Isaac Watts, "I Sing the Mighty Power of God"

Lesson Four

The eternal and righteous Word contains over 400 references to song *and* at least 50 direct commands to sing! Often called "the Bible's hymnbook," the book of Psalms consists of over 100 pages of songs.

Songs are clearly important to God, so we're going to spend another day focusing on how and why we are to use song and music to worship our Creator. Plan to take two or more days to steep yourself in these passages. If a song comes to your mind while reading these various passages, take time to stop and sing to the Lord with your whole heart!

1 Look up the following verses. Write one or more observations from each passage regarding how we are instructed to use music in our worship. Our Lord commands us to sing:

1 Chronicles 16 _____

Psalm 33:1-3 _____

Psalm 92:1-4 _____

Isaiah 42:10-13 _____

Colossians 3:16 _____

Why are we to sing? Read one or more of these psalms to see many of the endless reasons we have to sing as children of the Most High!

Psalm 47 _____

Psalm 96 _____

Psalm 147:1-11 _____

In Exodus 15, Moses and the Israelites sang a *hymn* of praise to God, rejoicing in His miraculous intervention and deliverance as they crossed the Red Sea with Pharaoh's horses and chariots in pursuit.

In Deuteronomy 31:19-21, the Lord instructs Moses to write another song and "teach it to the people of Israel. Put it in their mouths, that this song may be a witness for me...to confront them as a witness ..."

This song is recorded in **Deuteronomy 31:30-32:43.**

Write down a few of your observations: _____

_____

_____

_____

2 When we sing, we follow our Savior's example:

Matthew 26:26-30

What was the occasion when Jesus sang with His disciples? _____

_____

Hebrews 2:10-12

*Who does the resurrected Messiah sing with in heaven?*_____

_____

3 Who does God exhort to sing His praises?

Isaiah 44:23; 49:13

Isaiah 55:12

Take a moment and picture in your mind what clapping trees and singing mountains might look and sound like!

4 Where do our songs originate?

Psalm 40:1-3

Isaiah 12

Our LORD God, our Salvation, reminds us that He is not only the One to give us a song, but *he is* our Song!

One day soon, we will see the face of our Savior and worship Him around His throne. All His people will join with His creation in singing the song of the Lamb.

"Where is God my Maker, Who gives songs in the night?"

Job 35:10

5 How well are we using our earthly days to practice for singing in Heaven's choir?

Are we able to say with the psalmist, "Your statutes (are) my song in the house of my sojourning" (Psalm 119:54), and "My tongue sing(s) of Your Word…" (Psalm 119:172)?

"And the ransomed of the Lord shall return and come to Zion with singing; Everlasting joy shall be upon their heads…"

Isaiah 35:10

Take some time to reflect on this question from Bob Kauflin:

> 66
>
> The question is, *Do you have a song?* If you've turned from your sins and trusted in the finished work of Christ, if you're forgiven and reconciled to God, then you have a song. It's a song of the redeemed, of those who have been rescued from the righteous wrath of God through the cross of Jesus Christ and are now called his friends. Once we were not a people, but now we are the people of God, and our singing together, every voice contributing, is one way we express that truth.[24]
>
> 99

What could it look like for us to make God's statutes our song while we sojourn here on earth?

_____

_____

_____

6 Read Revelation 5:8-14 and 15:1-3.

Worship the Lamb and sing a hymn of praise to the only One worthy of our adoration, the only One qualified to ransom you and cover you with His robe of righteousness. Our ability to sing is not dependent upon us having a happy day but upon the fact that He has taken care of our greatest need and has already completed for us what we could never accomplish.

"I Sing the Mighty Power of God"
Isaac Watts

I sing the mighty pow'r of God, that made the mountains rise,
That spread the flowing seas abroad and built the lofty skies.
I sing the wisdom that ordained the sun to rule the day;
The moon shines full at His command, and all the stars obey.

I sing the goodness of the Lord, who filled the earth with food,
Who formed the creatures through the Word, and then pronounced them good.
Lord, how Thy wonders are displayed, where'er I turn my eye,
If I survey the ground I tread, or gaze upon the sky.

There's not a plant or flow'r below, but makes Thy glories known,
And clouds arise, and tempests blow, by order from Thy throne;
While all that borrows life from Thee is ever in Thy care;
And everywhere that we can be, Thou, God, art present there.

"Oh sing to the LORD a new song,
For he has done marvelous things!
… He has remembered his steadfast love
And faithfulness …"

Psalm 98:1,3

"I will sing of steadfast love and justice;
To You, O LORD, I will make music."

Psalm 101:1

"I will sing of the steadfast love of the LORD, forever;
With my mouth I will make known
your faithfulness to all generations."

Psalm 89:1

Lesson Five

During Lesson Two, we looked at our tendency to wander, to fail in our resolves even on our best days. Sadly, our love toward God can be fickle, our affections lukewarm, and our efforts to obey plagued with inconsistencies. This is all in stark contrast to our Shepherd, who is unwavering in His love; passionate and steady in His affections; and constant and loyal in His actions.

In this lesson, we are going to consider God's unchanging, perfect, stubborn, active, loyal, steadfast love. We'll look at just how regularly the Word instructs the children of God to sing of this love.

The Hebrew word *hesed* captures several of these amazing characteristics of God's steadfast love toward His sheep. His resolve to love us has stood firm since before time began. His covenant promise to love His sheep will continue on through eternity. Due to the important implications of God's steadfast love, plan to spend two or more days on this lesson. Given the infinite scope and inexhaustibility of God's *hesed* love, we will also spend time studying this topic in Lesson Eight, the final lesson in this study.

1 **Read Psalm 119, beginning in verse 41 through 160.** Highlight each time you see "steadfast love." Jot down the phrases that talk about "steadfast love."

_____

_____

_____

"Whoever is wise, let him attend to these things; let them consider the steadfast love of the Lord."

Psalm 107:43

From these specific verses, write a few sentences about your observations.

*God's steadfast love:*_____

_____

_____

_____

> **Steadfast:** resolutely firm and unwavering.
>
> *Synonyms:* loyal, committed, true, constant.
>
> *Antonyms:* disloyal, fickle, inconstant, unfaithful, untrue, traitorous.[25]

You may recall that "steadfast" is first used in verse 5 of Psalm 119. The psalmist expresses a desire that his "ways may be steadfast in keeping Your statutes." This is the one occasion in Psalm 119 where a different Hebrew word is used for steadfast. *Kun* is used here and it means "to be established, be firm, be prepared, be attached." The psalmist's plea is that his ways would be attached to *His* ways!

According to the *NIV Key Word Study Bible*, the Hebrew word *hesed* is used in verses 41, 64, 76, 88, 124, 149, and 159 of Psalm 119.

Here's a simple definition of *hesed*: unfailing love, loyal love, devotion, kindness.

The term translated "steadfast love" in the ESV and RSV is defined this way in other translations:

◊ "Faithful love" in CEB and CSB

◊ "Lovingkindnesses" in ASV and NASB

◊ "Mercies" in KJV

◊ "Unfailing love" in NIV and NLT

◊ "Loving devotion" in BSB

The Hebrew word *hesed* cannot be accurately described using just one English word. In our English language, this wonderfully complex word requires many different words put together to adequately convey the whole meaning. Here is how my friend Andrea Patterson describes God's *hesed* love:

> It's hard to capture the full meaning of hesed in English, but if we combine all of those translations, we can come close. 'Steadfast' means resolutely firm and unwavering; firmly fixed in place; not subject to change. 'Kindness' means favor, affection, or the state of being sympathetic, helpful, and forbearing; 'kindness' also implies deeds (you 'do someone a kindness'). 'Mercy' means compassion or forbearance; a blessing that is an act of divine favor. And 'love,' according to Merriam Webster, is 'a strong affection for another arising out of personal ties; a warm attachment, enthusiasm, or devotion; unselfish loyal and benevolent concern for the good of another.' *So hesed is an unwavering, unchanging, sympathetic, forbearing, devoted affection, worked out in deeds.* [emphasis mine].[26]

2 Let's dig deeper into what this psalm as well as the whole of Scripture teaches us about God's *hesed* love.

In Psalm 119:64, the psalmist declares, "The earth, O LORD, is full of your steadfast love…"

Psalm 33:5 states the same truth: "…the earth is full of the steadfast love of the Lord."

In Exodus 34:6-7, the Lord describes Himself as "a God merciful and gracious, slow to anger, and abounding in steadfast love and faithfulness, keeping steadfast love for thousands…" In this passage, the Lord connects His steadfast love with His faithfulness. This is a common connection throughout the Bible.

In what specific ways does this connection between God's steadfast love and His faithfulness make a difference in your thinking and your actions today?

As we study further, we will see that the Word often connects the steadfast love of God with other amazing attributes of our God.

From the following passages, which other attributes of God are connected to His *hesed* love?

Psalm 85:10-13_____

_____

_____

Psalm 36:5-10_____

_____

_____

Upon whom does God choose to pour out this *hesed* love?

Deuteronomy 5:10_____

_____

_____

Psalm 86:5_____

_____

_____

Psalm 103:17-18_____

_____

_____

"The basic concept for comfort in both the Old and New Testaments is encouragement, whether by words or the presence of another to help in time of need. Synonymous words are console, help, give relief, cheer up, exhort, and fear not."

Biblestudytools.com

3 In verse 76 of Psalm 119, the psalmist makes this request: "Let your steadfast love comfort me according to your promise…"

I recently learned that the final 26 chapters of Isaiah are often referred to as the volume, or book, of comfort. In Isaiah 51:12, God declares that He is the Author of comfort!

Read Isaiah 51:3-6,12-16 and Isaiah 54:4-10

What specific actions does the Lord of Hosts exercise here in order to comfort His people?

What promises does the Holy One make regarding His steadfast love?

Read Isaiah 61:1-9

How does our Savior bring comfort through His actions?

Looking back to the paragraph where Andrea defines hesed, *where and how do you see God's steadfast love demonstrating sympathy, forbearance, and/or compassion in these passages from Isaiah?*

4 How are we to respond to this tenacious, merciful love?

With thanksgiving:

"Oh give thanks to the Lord, for he is good,
For his steadfast love endures forever!"

Psalm 107:1

"And give thanks to the God of gods, for his steadfast love endures forever."

Psalm 136:2

With singing:

"My tongue will sing of your word…"

Psalm 119:172

"I will sing of the steadfast love of the LORD, forever…"

Psalm 89:1

"Oh sing to the LORD a new song, for he has done marvelous things! … He has remembered his steadfast love and faithfulness…"

Psalm 98:1, 3

"By day the LORD commands his steadfast love, and at night his song is with me."

Psalm 42:8

With love for others: **Read 1 John 4:7-12.**

5 To conclude this lesson and chapter, **read Psalm 138.**

Allow the reality of God's steadfast love to draw you into worship through grateful prayers and songs.

Praying: consider including in your prayers the following thoughts and questions:

◊ In what specific ways do you desire God to forbear with you, to stand alongside you?

◊ Where do you need His comfort and His encouragement to love and obey Him?

◊ Thank Him for personal, specific ways He has revealed His unwavering love and commitment to you.

◊ Praise Him for specific ways His love is a comfort to you today.

Singing: exalt Him with your own composition of a praiseful song, or find a hymn or worship song that articulates what's on your mind and heart.

And remember this: we are never singing alone. Jesus is singing God's praises with us (Hebrews 2:12)!

"Sing of the ways of the Lord..."
Psalm 138:5

"May the Lord direct your hearts to the love of God and to the steadfastness of Christ."
2 Thessalonians 3:5

Excerpted from "The Stability of His Steadfast Love (Psalm 33)"

By Sam Storms

> For anyone who reads the Psalms, the answer is obvious. The only thing in life or death that merits our trust is *God's love.* The dollar may rise or fall, nations may totter on the brink of destruction, a spouse may prove unfaithful, but through it all the confidence of the child of God ought to remain constant and unaffected, because God's love never fails.
>
> Three times in Psalm 33 we are told about God's "steadfast" (ESV) or "unfailing love" (NIV; "lovingkindness" in the NASB). When everything and everyone else bottoms out, the psalmist assures us that "the earth is full of the

steadfast love of the Lord" (v. 5). The eyes of the Lord, he tells us, are "on those who hope in his steadfast love" (v. 18). His prayer gets right to the point: "Let your steadfast love, O Lord, be upon us, even as we hope in you" (v. 22).......

That's what Psalm 33 is all about. It was written to remind you and me that there is one refuge that is impenetrable to disappointment and betrayal. You may think you're all out of confidence, but what little you've got left, invest in the unfailing love of an undying God…...

What we now know about God and his unfailing love calls for loud and jubilant exultation, not because God is hard of hearing, but because the psalmist knows it is natural for people to rejoice loudly in that which they find most delightful.

We are to sing to God a "new song." Why? Because every time we gather as the body of Christ to worship we have new and fresh reasons to sing! "You'll never believe what God did for me yesterday!" "Oh yes I will. But first let me tell you what I learned about God's character from Romans!"

With God there's always a fresh display of goodness and grace. Each day brings a new and more powerful manifestation of his greatness and mercy. God himself creates the need for new songs by granting new insight into his works and ways. He is constantly doing new and fresh things for which we need new and fresh declarations in song! Praise God for his steadfast love!

To read more, go to https://www.samstorms.com/all-articles/ post/the-stability-of-his-steadfast-love--psalm-33- *Or QR code at right*

Chapter Eight

Psalm 119

"You have established the earth, and it stands fast. By your appointment they stand this day, for all things are your servants."

Psalm 119:90b-91

"...my heart stands in awe of your words."

Psalm 119:161b

Stand: *to support oneself on the feet in an erect position; to rise to an erect position; to take up or maintain a specified position or posture; to maintain one's position; to be in a particular state or situation.*

Note

Throughout the writing of this study, the following quotes have been my companions:

"Psalm 119 opens doors into the rest of Scripture."[1]

"Psalm 119 carries you outside of itself to the rest of God's revelation and to all of life."[2]

"Take a verse of Psalm 119 every morning to meditate upon, and so go over the Psalm twice in a year: and that … will bring you to be in love with all the rest of the Scriptures."[3]

To continue growing in knowing, loving, and standing on God's inerrant and active Word—what a worthy prayer and pursuit this is! With that in mind, let's take one more chapter to allow Psalm 119 to open new doors for us into all the rest of Scripture and spur us on to love it more.

> "Your statutes, LORD, stand firm; holiness adorns your house for endless days" (Psalm 93:5, NIV).

> The Statutes of our God stand firm. All of His promises in Christ are yes and amen (2 Corinthians 1:20)!

> "Be watchful, stand firm in the faith…" (1 Corinthians 16:13a).

> "Therefore take up the whole armor of God, that you may be able to withstand in the evil day, and having done all, to stand firm. Stand therefore, having fastened on the belt of truth, and having put on the breastplate of righteousness…" (Ephesians 6:13-14a).

To gain the most from this chapter, go slowly. Take two or more days to cover each lesson.

Store: Choose your favorite stanza from all of Psalm 119 and begin storing it up in your heart and mind. Spend time each day committing the stanza to memory.

Sit at the feet of Jesus. Take time to *savor* and *steep* yourself in God's precious truths. Conclude your daily time of *study* with prayers of praise, *supplication*, and *surrender. Sing* to God, worshiping your LORD and Savior. Choose from the suggested prayers and songs or write your own. And then, *stand* up, ready "to walk in a manner worthy of the Lord, fully pleasing to Him, bearing fruit in every good work and increasing in the knowledge of God" (Colossians 1:10).

Heavenly Father give us eyes to see Your glory.

Holy Spirit, affect us and change us
as we study, delight in, and stand on Your testimonies.

Jesus, may our awe and wonder of You continue to
grow, as we look for Your Presence on every page.

*"If you have prayer on one hand, have praise on the other.
The mixture of these two perfumes
will make an exceedingly sweet incense unto the Lord."[4]*

Charles Spurgeon

*"The best possible praise is that which proceeds from men who honour God,
not only with their lips, but in their lives.
We learn the music of heaven in the school of holy living.
He whose life honours the Lord is sure to be a man of praise."[5]*

Charles Spurgeon

Lesson One

Read Psalm 119:1-32

1 Choose one or more verses from today's passage to *study, love,* and *get on speaking terms* with. Write it out here:

_____

_____

_____

Ask God to open your eyes to see "wondrous things" (v. 18).

Where do you need Psalm 119 to "befriend you" (as David Powlison said)?

_____

_____

> "When we get on speaking terms with a single verse, we begin to understand something of where the entire psalm intends to take us."[6]
>
> **David Powlison**

> "Take the specific sayings of God and learn to love them one by one."[7]
>
> **James Montgomery Boice**

A few suggestions for learning to love and get on speaking terms with a single verse:

◊ Slowly read the verse out loud several times, each time emphasizing a different word.

◊ Look up the verse in several different reliable translations. Biblestudytool.com is a good website for this purpose.

◊ Pray through the verse, talking with and listening to the Lord.

◊ Write the verse on an index card and post where you can see it regularly (for example, above your kitchen or bathroom sink or next to the trackpad on your laptop).

◊ Find your verse in a reliable commentary and learn from what godly scholars have said about it. Here are a few suggestions:

  • "Top 5 Commentaries on the Book of Psalms" from Ligonier Ministries, ligonier.org/blog/top-5-commentaries-on-the-book-of-psalms/

  • The list of commentaries on biblestudytools.com/commentaries

  • The list of commentaries on biblegateway.com/resources/commentaries

66 Now...the first thing I did, after having asked in a few words the Lord's blessing upon His precious Word, was, to begin to meditate on the Word of God, searching, as it were, into every verse, to get blessing out of it....The result I have found to be almost invariably this, that after a very few minutes my soul has been led to confession, or to thanksgiving, or to intercession, or to supplication...[8] 99

George Mueller

✣ This Lesson's Focus: LORD

2 You have probably noticed that every time the psalmist refers to God as Lord in Psalm 119, the entire word LORD is capitalized. From today's selected verses, you will find this in verses 1, 12, and 31.

"Blessed are You, O LORD."

(v. 12a)

Following are several definitions of the name "LORD":

"Yahweh is the promised name of God. This name of God which is too holy to voice, is actually spelled Yhwh. Yhwh is referred to as the Tetragrammaton (which simply means the four letters)."[9]

"Scripture speaks of the Tetragrammaton as 'this glorious and fearful name'... It connotes God's nearness, His concern for men and the revelation of His redemptive covenant."[10]

"Yahweh is used when God's covenantal relationship with Israel is in view."[11]

"Yhwh is parallel to I am who I am. Personal, eternal and all-sufficient."[12]

Oh, the splendors of our personal, glorious, covenantal, and awe-inspiring God! In this lesson, we are specifically focusing on the Lord's nearness—His personal commitment to and with each of His children. (In Lesson Three we will focus on the covenantal aspect of our Lord.)

Look up Deuteronomy 4:1-8

According to Moses, what distinctives set the Israelites apart from other nations? _____

_____

_____

Isaiah 40:10-11

List the specific actions of our God. Notice the contrasts in His character: _____

_____

_____

Seen together, these vastly varied actions of our God display a beautiful picture of Who our God is. He rules with absolute power and might, and yet He gently and lovingly gathers us in His arms.

3 Oh, the nearness of our glorious God! How is His nearness described in the following verses?

Psalm 145:18 _____

_____

_____

Matthew 1:23 _____

_____

_____

Galatians 2:20 _____

_____

_____

Revelation 3:20 _____

_____

_____

66   But You are near, O LORD, and all your commandments are true.   99

   Psalm 119:151

4 Read and meditate on one of the following Psalms. Jot down a few specific phrases that demonstrate God's personal care for you, and marvel at further evidence of His nearness.

Psalm 23 _____

_____

_____

Psalm 139

Sit at the feet of Jesus, taking time to pray, listen, and sing. Offer personal praises to your God, using specific truths about His nearness.

> Come down, O love divine,
> Seek thou this soul of mine,
> And visit it with thine own ardor glowing.
> O Comforter, draw near, within my heart appear,
> And kindle it, thy holy flame bestowing.[13]

Bianco da Siena

Song suggestion:

"Near The Cross" by Fanny J. Crosby

> Jesus, keep me near the cross,
> There a precious fountain
> Free to all, a healing stream,
> Flows from Calv'ry's mountain.
>
> Near the cross, a trembling soul,
> Love and Mercy found me;
> There the Bright and Morning Star
> Sheds its beams around me.
>
> Near the cross! O Lamb of God,
> Bring its scenes before me;
> Help me walk from day to day,
> With its shadows o'er me.
>
> *Refrain:*
> In the cross, in the cross,
> Be my glory ever;
> Till my raptured soul shall find
> Rest beyond the river.[14]

"But I have trusted in your steadfast love;
my heart shall rejoice in your salvation.
I will sing to the LORD,
Because He has dealt bountifully with me."

Psalm 13:5-6

"... We stand upon the Rock.
Let the sea rage; it cannot dissolve the Rock;
let the billows rise, they cannot sink the vessel of Jesus Christ."[15]

Saint John Chrysostom

"Behold, the eye of the LORD is on those who fear him,
On those who hope in his steadfast love,
That he may deliver their soul from death…"

Psalm 33:18-19a

Lesson Two

Read Psalm 119: 33-72

1 In his article "Suffering and Psalm 119," David Powlison states that Psalm 119 in its entirety is an "outcry of faith,"[16] "a rich confession of faith,"[17] and "faith in action."[18] In today's section of verses, note specifically where and how you see the psalmist...

Crying out for faith: _____

_____

_____

Confessing or declaring faith: _____

_____

_____

Acting in faith: _____

_____

_____

Today, do you find yourself in need of crying out to the Lord for faith as you walk through a trial? Or do you need to take a specific action of faith in order to be obedient? Take some time to talk with the Lord about this. Use specific verses to share your requests and declarations with Him.

❧ This Lesson's Focus: God's *hesed* love brings salvation.

Psalm 119:41 says "Let your steadfast love come to me, O LORD, your salvation according to your promise."

Charles Spurgeon explains verse 41 this way: "Salvation is joined with mercy; the sum and crown of all mercies—deliverance from all evil, both now and forever. What a mass of mercies are heaped together in the one salvation of our Lord Jesus!"[19]

2 The connection between God's steadfast love and His gift of salvation is not unique to this psalm. **Read Psalm 85 and Psalm 86** and notice the numerous connections between God's steadfast love and His gift of salvation.

Write out a few of these connections and take time to meditate on these truths: _____

_____

_____

"But now in Christ Jesus you who once were far off have been brought near by the blood of Christ. For he himself is our peace..."

Ephesians 2:13-14a

Looking at Psalms 85 and 86, as well as Psalm 119:33-72, what additional attributes of the LORD do you see that help us understand the scope of His hesed *love?*

"Righteousness and peace meet in Christ, God's man. ... they kissed each other on this [Christmas] day, because the gospel performed what the law promised."[20]

John Boys

_____

_____

Where do you see God's perfect and holy righteousness kissing (connecting with) His peace (Psalm 85:10)?

_____

_____

As we contemplate how salvation powerfully displays God's *hesed* love, here are a few thoughts from Tremper Longman in his commentary on Psalm 85:

> 66
>
> The psalmist ends with a powerful reflection on God's covenant with His people, personifying the divine qualities that are promised in the covenant and displayed in His relationship with His people. Steadfast love is the loyalty that the covenantal king demonstrated to his vassal people. Faithfulness affirms that God will indeed follow through on His promises. Righteousness indicates that God will act in accordance with His nature, and the harmony of peace is the result (a blessing of the covenant). Verse 10 presents the touching picture of these four qualities coming together in an intimate embrace in the person of God.[21]
>
> 99

3 Take time to savor the following verses that help explain this beautiful, awful place where God's *hesed* love and salvation meet. Notice the different words used to describe this multi-faceted love.

Psalm 130:7

"O Israel, hope in the LORD! For with the LORD there is steadfast love, and with him is plentiful redemption." (ESV)

"Israel, put your hope in the LORD, for with the LORD is unfailing love, and with Him is full redemption." (NIV)

"Israel, put your hope in the Lord. For there is faithful love with the Lord, and with Him is redemption in abundance." (CSB)

Romans 5:8

"...but God shows his love for us in that while we were still sinners, Christ died for us." (ESV)

"But God demonstrates his own love for us in this: While we were still sinners, Christ died for us." (NIV)

"But God proves His own love for us in that while we were still sinners, Christ died for us." (CSB)

The steadfast *(hesed)* love of our faithful God, revealed in His salvation, is a firm foundation—one in which we can "take up and maintain" our total and final "position" (Psalm 18:2; Psalm 62:7).

How does God's steadfast love shown in salvation intersect with your present burdens, joys, thoughts, and actions?

_____

_____

_____

"...that though he was rich, yet for our sakes he became poor, so that through his poverty we might become rich."

2 Corinthians 8:9

"Salvation is an aggregate of mercies incalculable in number, priceless in value, incessant in application, eternal in endurance."[22]

Thank and praise God for loving us so much that He gave His only begotten Son.

Thank and praise Jesus for choosing to leave His rightful place in Heaven in order to bring salvation to all who believe, repent, and place their trust in Him.

"Calvary's Anthem," Valley of Vision

HEAVENLY FATHER,
Thou hast led me singing to the cross
where I fling down all my burdens
and see them vanish,
where my mountains of guilt are levelled
to a plain,
where my sins disappear, though they are
the greatest that exist,
and are more in number than the grains
of fine sand;
For there is power in the blood of Calvary
to destroy sins more than can be counted
even by one from the choir of heaven.
Thou hast given me a hill-side spring
that washes clear and white,
and I go as a sinner to its waters,
bathing without hindrance
in its crystal streams.
At the cross there is free forgiveness
for poor and meek ones,
and ample blessings that last forever;
The blood of the Lamb is like a great river
of infinite grace
with never any diminishing of its fullness
as thirsty ones without number drink of it.
O Lord, forever will thy free forgiveness live
that was gained on the mount of blood;
In the midst of a world of pain
it is a subject for praise in every place,
a song on earth, an anthem in heaven,
its love and virtue knowing no end.
I have a longing for the world above
where multitudes sing the great song,
for my soul was never created to love
the dust of earth.
Though here my spiritual state is frail and poor,
I shall go on singing Calvary's anthem.
May I always know
that a clean heart full of goodness

is more beautiful than the lily,
that only a clean heart can sing by night
and by day,
that such a heart is mine when I abide
at Calvary.[23]

Song suggestions:

"The Lord is my Salvation" by Keith and Kristyn Getty

"My Living Hope" by Phil Wickham

"And Can It Be That I Should Gain" by Charles Wesley, 1738

> And can it be that I should gain
> An int'rest in the Savior's blood?
> Died He for me, who caused His pain?
> For me, who Him to death pursued?
> Amazing love! how can it be,
> That Thou, my God, shouldst die for me?
> ...He left His Father's throne above,
> So free, so infinite His grace;
> Emptied Himself of all but love,
> And bled for Adam's helpless race;
> 'Tis mercy all, immense and free;
> For, O my God, it found out me!
> Amazing love! How can it be,
> That Thou, my God, shouldst die for me?

"In order to grow in grace, we must be much alone with God.
It is not in society, even Christian society that the soul grows most rapidly
and vigorously.
In one single quiet hour of prayer it will often make more progress than in
whole days of company with others."²⁴

Horatius Bonar, Ministerial Confessions

"O beloved! I can say for myself, I am a continual miracle of divine grace.
If thou leave me, Lord, for a moment, I am utterly undone."²⁵

Charles Spurgeon, Spurgeon's Sermons vol 5

Lesson Three

As we learned in Lesson Seven, Psalm 119 is a wisdom psalm. As Longman explains, "The wisdom psalms call us to be wise, to be righteous, to follow the law of God. As we receive this command, it draws us to Jesus. …. we can't be wise ourselves. We must seek wisdom elsewhere. We find it only in the person of Jesus Christ…"[26]

Longman continues:

> After interpreting a psalm according to its Old Testament context, consider how the psalm anticipates the coming of Jesus Christ. Ask how the song may be sung to Jesus.[27]

1 **Read Psalm 119:73-104.** As you read the Psalm, take time to look for Jesus, "in whom are hidden all the treasures of wisdom and knowledge" (Colossians 2:3).

Where might one or more of these verses be a witness to the coming of the Messiah?

Where do you see Jesus' presence or His example on display?

Is there a particular verse that draws you to Jesus—your wise, humble, righteous, and loving Savior?

_____

_____

Is there a particular song you want to sing to Jesus in light of these verses? _____

_____

_____

Answer this question, which Sinclair Ferguson believes we should ask of every psalm: "How and when might these words have been on Jesus' mind?"

_____

_____

During my first read-through, I had trouble answering these questions. I had to slow down and ask God to open my eyes. I then read one verse at a time, and I began to see!

For example, verse 75b says, "In faithfulness You have afflicted me." I remembered that God the Father afflicted His own beloved Son in faithfulness; why, then, do I often think I should be exempted from affliction? I recalled a verse that says something like "it was the Father's will to crush Him." I looked up "crush" in the back of my Bible and found Isaiah 53:10. That caused me to read all of Isaiah 53 and offer praise to my Savior for how His affliction brought my salvation.

Verses 89-91 speak of God's eternal presence. As we learned in a previous lesson, Jesus was with God from before the beginning of time; so I realized these verses are not only speaking of God the Father, but of Jesus, God the Son. I wanted to find additional verses that speak of this truth, so I grabbed my phone and looked up the phrase "Jesus was with God from the beginning." The first item that popped up was an article by John Piper entitled "Before Time Began, Jesus Was," from *Desiring God*, October 11, 2017. I looked up a few of the verses used in the article. My gaze and my soul were lifted upward as I meditated on these truths about my Savior. I was motivated to see more of His Presence in Psalm 119.

Keep in mind that there are no specific "right answers" to these questions. However, developing eyes that "look for Jesus" will cause our awe and wonder at Jesus to grow, and our love and delight in His Word to blossom.

This Lesson's Focus: God's steadfast (*hesed*) love is connected to and revealed in His covenant promises.

2 **Read verse 76**: "Let your steadfast love comfort me according to your promise to your servant." Here we see that God's steadfast love is linked to His covenants, and promises.

Look up the following passage to see further evidence of this connection.

Psalm 89:20-35

Here is how my pastor, Josh Fenska, defines YAHWEH, which explains this covenantal aspect of the LORD's name:

> YHWH (YAHWEH) is a divine name (*the* divine name) given to Moses and used all across the Old Testament. In almost all English translations, YHWH is represented with the word "LORD" in all caps. YHWH is a relational / covenantal name for the God-Who-IS. (In Ex. 3:13-15, YHWH is set alongside God explaining, "I AM WHO I AM.") It is not a generic name for any old deity (like the more generic Hebrew word *elohim*, usually translated "God"). It is not a distant concept (like we might associate with "a lord"). It is a name that is almost always tied specifically to His relationship with His covenant people. When you read the term LORD, you can very often find significance in considering how the covenant commitment of God (past, present and future) to His redeemed people shines light on what is being said.

"For the mountains may depart and the hills be removed, but my steadfast love shall not depart from you, and my covenant of peace shall not be removed,' says the LORD, who has compassion on you."

Isaiah 54:10

3 During this lesson, we will barely begin to dip our toes into the vast ocean of the covenant commitments of God. If you'd like to dig deeper, I encourage you to read or listen to John Piper's message, "The Covenant of Abraham," which you can find on www.desiringgod.org/messages/the-covenant-of-abraham or by scanning the QR code at right.

Look up the following passages and write down the covenant commitments of God.

Genesis 12:1-3 _____

_____

Genesis 13:14-17 _____

_____

Genesis 15: 1-6; 17-21 _____

_____

Genesis 17:1-8 _____

_____

Exodus 2:23-25 (or even through chapter 3) _____

_____

Joshua 21:43-45 _____

_____

At the end of his life, Joshua makes this awesome declaration in Joshua 23:14b: "Not one word has failed of all the good things that the LORD your God promised concerning you. All have come to pass for you; not one of them has failed."

4 How do these Old Testament covenants apply to us, living in the 21st century? Here is how John Piper answers that question in "The Covenant of Abraham":

> "All this blessing promised to Abraham will be enjoyed someday by all the families of the earth. God's purpose is to bless the world with the blessings of Abraham. He is to be a conduit, not a cul-de-sac, of God's blessing. Genesis 12:2, 3, "I will bless you . . . so that you will be a blessing . . . and in you shall all the families of the earth be blessed" (cf. 18:18; 22:18). Therefore,

even though God has begun his redemptive, reclaiming process with a single individual, he has in view the world. He has a plan, a clear purpose for the centuries, and it reaches even to us...

God's 4,000-year-old relation to Abraham is of immense importance for your life as a believer today. Everything written about Abraham "was written for your instruction, that by steadfastness and by the encouragement of the scriptures you might have hope" (Romans 15:4)."[28]

The author of Psalm 119 seems to understand this connection between Abraham and himself:

> Let your steadfast love comfort me according to your promise to your servant (v.76).

Read Galatians 3:7-14; 23-29.

How can we know that God's covenantal promises are for us today? _____

_____

_____

_____

> So then, *those who have faith* are blessed *with* faithful Abraham...In Christ Jesus the blessing of Abraham comes upon the Gentiles, that we might receive the promise of the Spirit through faith (v.14) ...There is neither Jew nor Greek, there is neither slave nor free, there is neither male nor female; for you are all one in Christ Jesus. And if you are Christ's then you are Abraham's offspring (seed), heirs according to the promise (v.28,29) [emphasis added].[29]

Through faith, which is a gift from God, we are the beneficiaries of this covenantal, *hesed* love. By faith, we can and should place our complete hope in our gracious LORD and His covenantal promises.

"..but the LORD takes pleasure in those who fear Him, in those who hope in His steadfast love."

Psalm 147:11

"Let your steadfast love, O LORD, be upon us, even as we hope in You."

Psalm 33:22

"Know therefore that the LORD your God is God, the faithful God who keeps covenant and steadfast love with those who love Him and keep His commandments, to a thousand generations.

Deuteronomy 7:9

As you reflect on God's steadfast love, I recommend reading through this section of the prayer "Covenant Faithfulness," from *Prone to Wander: Prayers of Confession and Celebration.*

Faithful heavenly Father,

You are a covenant-keeping God, but we have forsaken your law and violated your statutes. We have not walked according to your rules or kept your commandments. Though you have always been faithful to us, we are unfaithful to you many times each day in our thoughts and with our words and actions. We know that we deserve to be punished for our sin. We have earned the rod of your anger and violent stripes of bitter anguish for our mountains of iniquity. Father, because of your steadfast love, forgive us we pray.

Jesus, you have been faithful in all things for us, keeping covenant with your Father on our behalf. You were the sinless Servant who kept the law perfectly, the perfect Son who walked according to your Father's commandments, and now you have become the Rock of our salvation. You truly earned the steadfast love and faithfulness of God, but willingly surrendered to the punishment that we deserve for all our rebellion. Instead of a throne here on earth, you chose a cross; instead of the honor of a high king, you chose the humiliation of whips and lashes, your flesh torn as you endured our stripes of anguish. You freely took our place, enduring our shame as you were lifted up to die. Thank you, Lord Jesus. Now the empty tomb proclaims God's faithfulness to you, his obedient Son, and to all of us who are united to you. By faith we behold you, the Holy Lamb of God, crowned with glory and honor and seated on a throne that will last forever. You are so worthy to be praised.[30]

Song suggestions:

"Before the Throne of God Above" by Charitie Lees Bancroft

> Before the throne of God above
> I have a strong and perfect plea:
> A great High Priest, whose name is Love,
> Who ever lives and pleads for me….
>
> Behold Him there, the Risen Lamb
> My perfect, spotless righteousness,
> The great unchangeable I am,
> The King of glory and of grace!

"Standing on the promises of Christ my King" by Russell Kelso Carter

> Standing on the promises of Christ my King,
> Thro' eternal ages let His praises ring;
> Glory in the highest, I will shout and sing,
> Standing on the promises of God.
>
> Standing on the promises, I cannot fall,
> List'ning every moment to the Spirit's call,
> Resting in my Savior as my all in all,
> Standing on the promises of God.

"… Let us offer to God acceptable worship,
with reverence and awe,
for our God is a consuming fire."

Hebrews 12:28-29

"Live your lives as strangers here in reverent fear."

1 Peter 1:17

"The fear of God in which godliness consists is the fear which
constrains (compels or powerfully produces) adoration and love.
It is the fear which consists in awe, reverence, honor, and
worship, and all of these on the highest level of exercise.
It is the reflex in our consciousness of the transcendent
majesty and holiness of God."[31]

John Murray

Lesson Four

Read Psalm 119:105-144

 This Lesson's Focus: fearing God = obedience + awe

1 Consider the contrast between fear and wonder in the following verses:

"My flesh trembles for fear of you, and I am afraid of your judgments" (v.120).

"Your testimonies are wonderful; therefore my soul keeps them" (v.129).

Spurgeon explains the connection between the wonder of God's ways and the psalmist's obedience this way: "Their wonderful character so impressed itself upon his mind that he kept them in his memory; their wonderful excellence so charmed his heart that he kept them in his life."[32]

How are we to think appropriately about a God who is both loving and yet perfect in holiness? How are we to respond to this God who is both near yet to be feared, Abba and Yahweh, our loving Shepherd and a "consuming fire" and "a jealous god" (Deuteronomy 4:24)?

Here is how several theologians describe the fear of the Lord:

◊ "True religion consists in a proper mixture of fear of God, and of hope in his mercy; and wherever either of these is entirely wanting, there can be no true religion. Those only who both fear him and hope in his mercy, give him the honour that is due to his name" (Edward Payson). [33]

◊ "That indefinable mixture of reverence, fear, pleasure, joy and awe which fills our heart when we realize who God is and what He has done for us."[34]

◊ Jerry Bridges uses the term "reverential awe." He defined awe as "an emotion in which dread, veneration, and wonder are variously mingled."[35] To have a proper fear of God, "we need to include respect (which toward God means reverence) in recognition of His infinite worth and dignity; admiration of His glorious attributes; and amazement at His infinite love."[36]

"Let all the earth fear the LORD; let all the inhabitants of the world stand in awe of him!"

Psalm 33:8

The following passages are just two examples of the many Scriptures that speak about this mixture of fear, awe, and obedience. The passage from Malachi is a sober reminder that our God does not ignore dishonor to His name.

1 Samuel 12:24

Malachi 2:1-9

2 From the verses below, what are additional ways we demonstrate appropriate biblical fear of God?

Exodus 14:31 _____

_____

_____

_____

Deuteronomy 6:1-25 _____

_____

_____

Joshua 24:14 _____

_____

_____

_____

"The end of the matter;
all has been heard.
Fear God and keep his
commandments,
for this is the whole duty
of man."

Ecclesiastes 12:13

Psalm 33:18 _____

_____

_____

_____

3 From the connections we've seen between fear/trust/hope/awe/obedience, look for examples in **Psalm 119:105-144** and record your observations.

Note where you see the psalmist fearing God by…

Hoping and trusting in His mercy: _____

_____

_____

Standing in awe of God's character and what He has done: _____

_____

_____

Obeying His words of life: _____

_____

_____

Read Isaiah 11:1-3 to see the ultimate example of one who delights in fearing the LORD.

> 66   None reverence the Lord more than they who know him best and are most familiar with him.[37]   99
>
> *William Cowper*

"The friendship of the LORD is for those who fear him, and he makes known to them his covenant."

Psalm 25:14

"The fear of the LORD is a fountain of life, that one may turn away from the snares of death."

Proverbs 14:27

"Oh, how abundant is your goodness, which you have stored up for those who fear you and worked for those who take refuge in you, in the sight of the children of mankind!"

Psalm 31:19

Through His living and active Word, God promises *many* rewards for those who fear Him. Oh, the kindness and generosity of our God!

4   As you take time to talk with the LORD, complete the following sentences:

I have the opportunity to fear God when I trust Him with…

_____

_____

I fear God as I consider, declare and praise Him for these great and specific things He has done for me:

_____

_____

I fear God when I resist the specific sin of _____ *and obey Him by…*

_____

_____

66 We… will trust God to the extent we fear Him; to the extent we stand in absolute awe and amazement at His great power and sovereign rule over all His creation. Frequent meditation on passages of Scripture such as Isaiah 40 will help us fear the Lord and be able to trust Him more.[38] 99

For more reflection, see prayer and songs on the next page.

Prayer:

Glorious God,
It is the flame of my life to worship thee,
the crown and glory of my soul to adore thee,
heavenly pleasure to approach thee.
Give me power by thy Spirit to help me worship now,
that I may forget the world,
be brought into fullness of life,
be refreshed, comforted, blessed.
Give me knowledge of thy goodness
that I might not be over-awed by thy greatness;
Give me Jesus, Son of Man, Son of God,
that I might not be terrified,
but be drawn near with filial love,
with holy boldness;
He is my mediator, brother, interpreter,
branch, daysman, Lamb;
him I glorify,
in him I am set on high.
Crowns to give I have none,
but what thou hast given I return,
content to feel that everything is mine when it is thine,
and the more fully mine when I have yielded it to thee.
Let me live wholly to my Saviour,
free from distractions,
from carking care,

from hindrances to the pursuit of the narrow way.
I am pardoned through the blood of Jesus —
give me a new sense of it,
continue to pardon me by it,
may I come every day to the fountain,
and every day be washed anew,
that I may worship thee always in spirit and truth.[39]

Valley of Vision, "Worship"

Song suggestions:

Holy, Holy, Holy!...
Only Thou art holy;
There is none beside Thee,
Perfect in power,
In love, and purity.
Holy, holy, holy!
Lord, God Almighty!
All Thy works shall praise Thy name,
In earth and sky and sea;
Holy, holy, holy!
Merciful and mighty!
God in three persons, blessed Trinity!

"Holy, Holy, Holy" by Reginald Heber, John Bacchus Dykes, Public Domain

Come, Thou Almighty King,
Help us Thy Name to sing,
Help us to praise!
Father, all glorious, O'er all victorious,
Come and reign over us,
Ancient of Days!

To Thee, great One in Three,
Eternal praises be
Hence, evermore;
Thy sov'reign majesty
May we in glory see,
And to eternity
Love and adore!

"Come, Thou Almighty King" by Charles Wesley, 1757

*"Christ, the blessed One,
gives to all,
Wonderful words of life..."*

"Wonderful Words of Life"
by Philip P. Bliss, 1874

*"Amen!
Blessing and glory and wisdom and thanksgiving
and honor and power and might
Be to our God forever and ever!
Amen."*

Revelation 7:12

Lesson Five

1   **Read Psalm 119: 145-176** and:

*Look for Jesus! Where do you see His imprint?*_____

_____

_____

Choose a verse from today's passage to study, love, and get on speaking terms with. Use one or more of the suggestions from Lesson Two.

_____

_____

Use the prayers and songs of the psalmist in these stanzas and make them your own. _____

_____

_____

List where and how do you need to...

Cry out for faith: _____

_____

_____

Confess faith: _____

_____

_____

Stand on His Promises: _____

_____

_____

Act in faith: _____

_____

_____

Find one affirmation about God and His Word that you need to see, believe, and declare. Speak truth to yourself about your God.

What step of obedience can you take today to declare your trust in Him and His Word?

_____

_____

_____

This Lesson's Focus: God's steadfast *hesed* love= life!

2 Consider the following verses:

"In your steadfast love give me life…" (v. 88).

"Give me life according to your steadfast love" (v.159).

Ironically, in order to understand the connection between God's *hesed* love and life, we must first discuss death. In his book *A Loving Life*, Paul Miller offers this definition of *hesed*:

> *Hesed*, a word unique to Hebrew that combines love and loyalty; a commitment with sacrifice. One-way love. Love without an exit strategy. Stubborn love. Unbalanced. Uneven. Unfair. Active. Not dependent upon or determined by feelings. When you love with *hesed* love, you bind yourself to the object of your love, no matter what the response is. Your response to the other person is entirely independent of how that person has treated you. Death is at the center of *hesed* love. That's why, subconsciously, we are allergic to love. We rightly sense that death is at the center of love.[40]

"Jesus's *hesed* of us means that he turns his face to the cross and never looks back."[41]

Paul Miller

3 Read the following passages. Take time to savor Jesus, His obedient death on your behalf, and the life that His death brings to you.

Ephesians 2:4-7

Philippians 2:5-11

1 John 4:9-1

1 Thessalonians 5:9-10

"Now it came to pass, when the time had come for Him to be received up, that He steadfastly set His face to go to Jerusalem."

Luke 9:51 (NKJV)

"By this we know love, that He laid down His life for us…"

1 John 3:16

4 Read the following passages and circle or highlight each time you see the word "life." Then write down the names or titles of Jesus that are used in these passages.

John 1:1-5 _____

John 6:35-51 _____

John 14:6 _____

One path leads to God and it is through Jesus, "the radiance of the glory of God" (Hebrews 1:3).

One path leads to life and it is through Jesus, "the image of the invisible God" (Colossians 1:15).

Jesus, the Way, the Truth, and the only Source of Life, invites us to come eat with Him at "the marriage supper of the Lamb" (Revelation 19:9)!

"Come, everyone who thirsts, come to the waters; and he who has no money, come, buy and eat! Come, buy wine and milk without money and without price."

Isaiah 55:1
(emphasis added)

Incline your ear, and come to me; *hear,* that your soul may *live;* and I will make with you an everlasting covenant, my steadfast, sure love for David.

Isaiah 55:3
(emphasis added)

The deceitful enemy of our present world is touting the lie that many paths lead to God and life. These passages, and countless others, expose that lie.

Read Jesus' appeal to all people in the final chapters of His eternal love letter:

Revelation 21:5-7

Revelation 22

To whom does the Alpha and Omega give this water of life?

_____

_____

What do we need to bring in order to receive it?

_____

_____

May the prayers and praises of the psalmist be our continual prayers and praises until the day Jesus calls us to our eternal Home.

"May the LORD direct your hearts to the love of God and to the steadfastness of Christ

2 Thessalonians 3:5

◊   "Give me life according to your Word" (Psalm 119:25b).

◊   "Give me life in Your ways" (Psalm 119:37b).

◊   "Let your mercy come to me, that I may live" (Psalm 119:77).

◊   "In your steadfast love give me life" (Psalm 119:88a).

◊   "Uphold me according to your promise, that I may live" (Psalm 119:116a).

◊   "Give me understanding that I may live" (Psalm 119:144b).

◊   "O LORD, according to your justice give me life" (Psalm 119:149b).

◊   "Give me life according to your steadfast love" (Psalm 119:159b).

May we live every day with the attitude of Simon Peter, who said to Jesus, "Lord, to whom shall we go? You have the words of eternal life" (John 6:68).

Come to the "Bread of Life" (John 6:35)! His arms are open wide. His heart is eager to embrace you.

Worship and bow down at the feet of the "Word of God," the "Fountain of Living Waters," "King of Kings and Lord of Lords" (Revelation 19, Jeremiah 2:13; 17:13).

Jesus Christ, the covenant-keeping God, overflowing with *hesed* love for you, His beloved child, speaks this promise over you: "For this is the will of my Father, that everyone who looks on the Son and believes in Him should have eternal life, and I will raise him up on the last day" (John 6:40).

Yes and amen! Come, Lord Jesus.

Prayers:

"Grant, O God, of your mercy,
That we may come to everlasting life,
And there beholding your glory as it is,
May equally say:
Glory to the Father who created us,
Glory to the Son who redeemed us,
Glory to the Holy Spirit who sanctified us.
Glory to the most high and undivided Trinity,
Whose works are inseparable,
Whose kingdom without end abides,
From age to age, forever, Amen."

Augustine, 354-430[42]

Sovereign Father, every single time I begin to get a little antsy, anxious, or angry about national and international politics, you center my heart with the music of heaven. What did followers of Jesus need in the crazy-making chaos of first-century Rome? The same thing we followers of Jesus need in the crazy-making chaos of our twenty-first century global community. We need to sing your story. We need to sing our theology. We need to sing the gospel!

Hand me a harp today, Father. I'll gladly join the heavenly chorus singing the song of Moses—a song of your Exodus grace, deliverance from the bondage of Egypt, deliverance into a land of freedom. But I'll sing the song of the Lamb even louder! For Jesus has delivered us from sin and death, into the glorious freedom of the children of God, and Jesus will deliver us into the ultimate land of freedom--the new heaven and new earth!

I'll not be afraid of any human king, but I will fear you, Lord, for you alone are holy and you alone are good. As the gospel does its work in my heart, I pray my thoughts, words, and deeds will increasingly bring you glory. I pray in Jesus' sovereign and saving name. Amen.

Excerpted from Everyday Prayers by Scotty Smith[43]

Song suggestions:

Love divine, all loves excelling,
Joy of Heav'n to earth come down;
Fix in us thy humble dwelling;
All thy faithful mercies crown!
Jesus, Thou art all compassion,
Pure unbounded love Thou art;
Visit us with Thy salvation,
Enter every trembling heart.
Finish, then, Thy new creation;
Pure and spotless let us be;
Let us see Thy great salvation
Perfectly restored in Thee;
Changed from glory into glory,
Till in Heav'n we take our place,
Till we cast our crowns before Thee,
Lost in wonder, love, and praise.

"Love Divine, All Loves Excelling" by
Charles Wesley, 1747

Sing them over again to me,
Wonderful words of life,
Let me more of their beauty see,
Wonderful words of life;
Words of life and beauty
Teach me faith and duty.
Beautiful words, wonderful words,
Wonderful words of life;
Beautiful words, wonderful words,
Wonderful words of life.
Christ, the blessed One, gives to all
Wonderful words of life;
Sinner, list to the loving call,
Wonderful words of life;
All so freely given,
Wooing us to heaven.
Sweetly echo the Gospel call,
Wonderful words of life;
Offer pardon and peace to all,
Wonderful words of life;
Jesus, only Savior,
Sanctify us forever.

"Wonderful Words of Life" by Philip P.
Bliss, 1874

Acknowlegments

I am grateful for my dear husband, Tim, who supported and encouraged me from start to finish and patiently assisted me in all areas of technology. May our gracious God shine His face upon you and continue to give you life in His ways (Psalm 119:135, 37).

To my friends at Useful Group: James, Rachel, Miranda, and Angie, thank you for your patience, kindness, and expertise. It was my pleasure to work with you.

Many thanks to Jill and Rachel Poel for offering the gift of your time to share insightful suggestions and revisions. May He continue to give you understanding, that you may live (Psalm 119:144).

To my sweet friends and family members, I so appreciate your meaningful words of encouragement along the way. Thank you. Give them life, O Lord, according to Your Word (Psalm 119:107)!

End Notes

Introduction

1. C. H Spurgeon, *The Treasury of David: An Expository and Devotional Com mentary on the Psalms.* (Grand Rapids, Mich.: Baker Book House, 1981), 1.

2. Spurgeon, 3.

3. Spurgeon, 2.

4. David Powlison, "Suffering and Psalm 119," *The Journal of Biblical Counseling* Fall 2004 (n.d.).

5. Charles Bridges, *Exposition of Psalm CXIX* (Wentworth Press, 2019), 6–7.

6. John Piper, *When I Don't Desire God: How to Fight for Joy* (Wheaton, Ill: Crossway Books, 2004), 124.

7. Donald S Whitney, Ask Pastor John, December 31, 2015.

8. Kathleen Buswell Nielson, *Psalms: Songs along the Way* (Phillipsburg, N.J.: P & R Pub., 2009), xi.

9. Spurgeon, *The Treasury of David*, 2.

10. C. Austin Miles, *I Come to the Garden Alone*, 1912.

Chapter One

1. *Merriam-Webster*, s.v. "store (*v.*)," accessed July 24, 2019, https://www.merriam-webster.com/dictionary/store.

2. Kate B. Wilkinson, "May the Mind of Christ My Savior," n.d.

3. C. H Spurgeon, *The Treasury of David: An Expository and Devotional Commentary on the Psalms.* (Grand Rapids, Mich.: Baker Book House, 1981), 1.

4. Taken from the *ESV® Study Bible* (The Holy Bible, English Standard Version®), copyright ©2008 by Crossway, a publishing ministry of Good News Publishers. Used by permission. All rights reserved.

5. Tremper Longman, *How to Read the Psalms* (Downers Grove, Ill: InterVarsity Press, 1988), 65.

6. Jen Wilkin, *None Like Him: 10 Ways God Is Different from Us (and Why That's a Good Thing)* (Wheaton, Illinois: Crossway, 2016), 53.

7. Robert J. Morgan, *100 Bible Verses Everyone Should Know by Heart* (Nashville, Tenn: B&H Pub. Group, 2010), 7. Used with permission.

8. Morgan, 11. Used with permission.

9. Morgan, 21. Used with permission.

10. Morgan, 15. Used with permission.

11. Morgan, 17. Used with permission.

12. John Bunyan, *The Pilgrim's Progress* (ed. Barry Horner (North Brunswick, N.J., 1997), 72.

13. David Powlison, "Suffering and Psalm 119," *The Journal of Biblical Counseling* Fall 2004 (n.d.): 4.

14. Herbert Lockyer, *Psalms: A Devotional Commentary* (Grand Rapids, MI: Kregel, 1993), 542.

15. Robert Boyd Munger, *My Heart—Christ's Home*, 2010, 12–16, http://site.ebrary.com/id/10834829. Used with permission.

Chapter Two

1. Merriam-Webster, s.v. "supplicate (v.)," accessed July 24, 2019, https://www.merriam-webster.com/dictionary/supplicate.

2. John Piper, *When I Don't Desire God: How to Fight for Joy* (Wheaton, Ill: Crossway Books, 2004), 109.

3. Mike Bullmore, *Sermon: The Soul Satisfying Power of the Word, Psalm 119*, 2004.

4. David Powlison, "Suffering and Psalm 119," *The Journal of Biblical Counseling* Fall 2004 (n.d.): 4.

5. Powlison, 4.

6. J.I. Packer, *My Path of Prayer* (Worthing, West Sussex: Henry E. Walter, 1981), 56.

7. *Westminster Shorter Catachism Project* (Bible Presbyterian Church Online, n.d.).

8. Powlison, "Suffering and Psalm 119," 5, 6.

9. Powlison, 6.

10. John Piper, *Seeing and Savoring Jesus Christ* (Wheaton, Ill: Crossway Books, 2001), 23.

11. John Bunyan, *The Pilgrim's Progress* (ed. Barry Horner (North Brunswick, N.J., 1997).

12. Piper, *Seeing and Savoring Jesus Christ*, 70.

13. William Law, *A Serious Call to a Devout & Holy Life*, Pure Gold Classic (Alachua, FL: Bridge-Logos, 2008), 147.

14. Charles Bridges, *Psalm 119*, sixteenth (Titus Books, Kindle Edition, n.d.), 45.

15. Powlison, "Suffering and Psalm 119," 1.

16. John Piper, "Going Deep with God by Having Him Carry Our Loads," October 31, 2000.

17. Piper, *When I Don't Desire God*, 159.

18. Taken from the *ESV*® *Study Bible* (The Holy Bible, English Standard Version®), copyright ©2008 by Crossway, a publishing ministry of Good News Publishers. Used by permission. All rights reserved.

19. C. H Spurgeon, *The Treasury of David: An Expository and Devotional Commentary on the Psalms.* (Grand Rapids, Mich.: Baker Book House, 1981), 73.

20. Powlison, "Suffering and Psalm 119," 4.

Chapter Three

1. Piper, *Seeing and Savoring Jesus Christ*, 54, 55.

2. Wilkinson, "May the Mind of Christ My Savior."

3. *Merriam-Webster*, s.v. "study (*v.*)," accessed July 24, 2019, https://www.merriam-webster.com/dictionary/study.

4. Spurgeon, *The Treasury of David*, 178.

5. "K" in Rippon's Selection, 1787, *How Firm a Foundation*.

6. Powlison, "Suffering and Psalm 119," 14.

7. Justin Taylor, "A Teachable Spirit," *Tabletalk Magazine*

8. Piper, *Seeing and Savoring Jesus Christ*, 23–24.

9. Bridges, *Exposition of Psalm CXIX*, 134.

10. Boice, *Psalms*, 1005.

11. Piper, *When I Don't Desire God*, 116.

12. *Hebrew-Greek Key Word Study Bible*, 1947.

13. Piper, *When I Don't Desire God*, 123.

14. Spurgeon, *The Treasury of David*, 210.

Chapter Four

1. Martin Luther, Jaroslav Jan Pelikan, and Helmut T. Lehmann, *Luther's Works. 9: Lectures on Deuteronomy* (Saint Louis, Mo. u.a: Concordia Publ. House u.a, 1960), 24.

2. *Merriam-Webster*, s.v. "steep (*v.*)," accessed July 24, 2019, https://www.merriam-webster.com/dictionary/steep.

3. "The Path Laid By Prophets," *Apologetics Magazine*, n.d., 62.

4. *Autobiography of George Muller*, comp. Fred Bergen (London: J. Nisber Co., 1906), 152–54.

5. John Piper, "Desiringgod.Org," *Sermon: Meditate on the Word of the Lord Day and Night* (blog), January 3, 1999.

6. D. Martyn Lloyd-Jones, *Spiritual Depression; Its Causes and Cures*, n.d., 20–21.

7. John Piper, *When I Don't Desire God: How to Fight for Joy* (Wheaton, Ill: Crossway Books, 2004), 135.

8. Robert J. Morgan, *100 Bible Verses Everyone Should Know by Heart* (Nashville, Tenn: B & H Pub. Group, 2010), 35. Used with permission.

9. Rev. Isaac Watts, *Psalms, Hymns & Spiritual Songs* (London: Thomas Nelson, Paternoster Row, 1849), 4.

10. A.W. Pink, *The Sovereignty of God* (Gideon House Books, 2016), chap. 1.

11. Thomas O. Chisholm, *Great Is Thy Faithfulness*, 1923.

12. St. Anselm, *Proslogion*, n.d., chap. 26.

13. David Powlison, "Suffering and Psalm 119," *The Journal of Biblical Counseling* Fall 2004 (n.d.): 10.

14. Piper, *When I Don't Desire God*, 149.

Chapter Five

1. *Merriam-Webster*, s.v. "savor (v.)," accessed July 24, 2019, https://www.merriam-webster.com/dictionary/savor.

2. C. H Spurgeon, *The Treasury of David: An Expository and Devotional Commentary on the Psalms.* (Grand Rapids, Mich.: Baker Book House, 1981), 248.

3. crosswalk.com/faith. May 21, 2015

4. *The Book of Common Prayer*, 1979, pt. 64. Before Worship.

5. Taken from the *ESV® Study Bible* (The Holy Bible, English Standard Version®), copyright ©2008 by Crossway, a publishing ministry of Good News Publishers. Used by permission. All rights reserved.

6. Fanny Crosby, *To God Be the Glory*, 1875.

7. Charles Dickens, *Oliver Twist*, n.d., Ch. 2.

8. C. S. Lewis, *The Chronicles of Narnia. Book 2: The Lion, the Witch and the Wardrobe* (New York: HarperTrophy, 2005), 38, 44.

9. C. H Spurgeon, *The Treasury of David: An Expository and Devotional Commentary on the Psalms.* (Grand Rapids, Mich.: Baker Book House, 1981), 229.

10. Spurgeon, *The Treasury of David*, 250.

11. Richard Baxter, *The Cure of the Melancoly*, n.d., 282.

12. Taken from the *ESV® Study Bible* (The Holy Bible, English Standard Version®), copyright ©2008 by Crossway, a publishing ministry of Good News Publishers. Used by permission. All rights reserved.

13. Robert Robinson, *Come Thou Fount of Every Blessing*, 1757.

14. James Montgomery Boice, *Psalms*, Pbk. ed (Grand Rapids, Mich: Baker Books, 2005), 1033.

15. Oswald Chambers, *My Utmost for His Highest*, n.d., pt. December 1.

16. Jerry Bridges and Bob Bevington, *The Bookends of the Christian Life* (Wheaton, Ill: Crossway Books, 2009), 95–96.

17. Spurgeon, *The Treasury of David*, 249.

18. Spurgeon, *The Treasury of David*, 264.

19. Spurgeon, *The Treasury of David*, 266.

20. Spurgeon, *The Treasury of David*, 267.

21. Ada Habershon, *He Will Hold Me Fast*, 1906.

Chapter Six

1. *Merriam-Webster,* s.v. "surrender (*v.*)," accessed July 30, 2019, https://www.merriam-webster.com/dictionary/surrender.

2. T. E. Brown, *The Collected Poems of T. E. Brown* (Macmillan and Co., ltd, n.d.).

3. David Powlison, "Suffering and Psalm 119," *The Journal of Biblical Counseling* Fall 2004 (n.d.).

4. *Merriam-Webster,* s.v. "pharisee (*n.*)," accessed July 24, 2019, https://www.merriam-webster.com/dictionary/pharisee.

5. *Merriam-Webster,* s.v. "surrender (*v.*)," accessed July 24, 2019, https://www.merriam-webster.com/dictionary/surrender.

6. C. H Spurgeon, *The Treasury of David: An Expository and Devotional Commentary on the Psalms.* (Grand Rapids, Mich.: Baker Book House, 1981), 283.

7. Scotty Smith, "The Gospel Coalition," March 9, 2013.

8. Charles Noel Douglas, *Forty Thousand Quatations, Prose and Poetical: Choice Extracts on History*, Ebook, n.d., 1482.

9. Isaac Watts, *When I Survey the Wondrous Cross,* 1707.

10. Jan Karon, *Patches of Godlight: Father Tim's Favorite Quotes.* (New York: Penguin Books, 2002).

11. *Merriam-Webster,* s.v. "wonder (*n.*)," accessed July 24, 2019, https://www.merriam-webster.com/dictionary/wonder.

12. Spurgeon, *The Treasury of David*, 283.

13. Jen Wilkin, "Women, Trade Self-Worth for Awe and Wonder," *Desiring God* (blog), July 16, 2016.

14. Spurgeon, *The Treasury of David*, 297.

15. Jerry Bridges and Bob Bevington, *The Bookends of the Christian Life* (Wheaton, Ill: Crossway Books, 2009), 19.

16. Jerry Bridges and Bob Bevington, *The Great Exchange* (Crossway, 2007), 82.

17. Spurgeon, *The Treasury of David*, 297.

18. Trevin Wax, "Gospel Definitions," *Kingdom People* (blog), *The Gospel Coalition*, May 7, 2008.

19. Bridges and Bevington, *The Bookends of the Christian Life*, 26.

20. Bridges and Bevington, 26, 27.

21. Bridges and Bevington, 29.

22. Spurgeon, *The Treasury of David*, 313.

23. *The Commemorative Edition of the Works of John Bunyan*, vol. 2, n.d., 8.

Chapter Seven

1. *Merriam-Webster*, s.v. "sing (*v.*)," accessed July 30, 2019, https://www.merriam-webster.com/dictionary/sing.

2. C. H Spurgeon, *The Treasury of David: An Expository and Devotional Commentary on the Psalms.* (Grand Rapids, Mich.: Baker Book House, 1981), 244.

3. James Montgomery Boice, *Living by the Book: The Joy of Loving and Trusting God's Word ; Based on Psalm 119* (Grand Rapids, Mich: Baker Books, 1997), 85.

4. John Piper, *Desiringgod.Org*, 1981, Be Filled with the Spirit.

5. Spurgeon, *The Treasury of David*, 250.

6. Spurgeon, 346.

7. Spurgeon, 4.

8. James Montgomery Boice, *Psalms*, Pbk. ed (Grand Rapids, Mich: Baker Books, 2005), 1062.

9. Spurgeon, 355.

10. Spurgeon, 347.

11. Kathleen Buswell Nielson, *Psalms: Songs along the Way* (Phillipsburg, N.J.: P & R Pub., 2009), xi.

12. John Lennon, Paul McCartney, *Help! By The Beatles* (Sony?ATV Music Publishing LLC, 1965).

13. Spurgeon, *The Treasury of David*, 140.

14. Henry Wadsworth Longfellow, *Poem, The Day Is Done*, n.d.

15. Charles H. Spurgeon, *The Salt-Cellars* (Delmarva Publications, Inc., n.d.).

16. Tremper Longman, *How to Read the Psalms* (Downers Grove, Ill: InterVarsity Press, 1988), 24.

17. Longman, 26.

18. Longman, 30.

19. Longman, 31.

20. Longman, 32.

21. Longman, 34.

22. Longman, 32.

23. Mike Bullmore, *Sermon: The Praise-Producing Power of the Word, Psalm 119*, 2004.

24. "Merriam-Webster."

Chapter Eight

1. *Merriam-Webster*, s.v. "stand (*v.*)," accessed July 30, 2019, https://www.merriam-webster.com/dictionary/stand.

2. David Powlison, "Suffering and Psalm 119," *The Journal of Biblical Counseling* Fall 2004 (n.d.): 14.

3. Powlison, 7.

4. Charles Bridges, *Exposition of Psalm CXIX* (Wentworth Press, 2019), 6–7.

5. C. H. Spurgeon, *Sermons*, vol. 10, n.d.

6. C. H. Spurgeon, *The Treasury of David: An Expository and Devotional Commentary on the Psalms*. (Grand Rapids, Mich.: Baker Book House, 1981), 345.

7. Powlison, "Suffering and Psalm 119," 3.

8. James Montgomery Boice, *Living by the Book: The Joy of Loving and Trusting God's Word ; Based on Psalm 119* (Grand Rapids, Mich: Baker Books, 1997), 98.

9. *Autobiography of George Muller*, comp. Fred Bergen (London: J. Nisber Co., 1906), 152–54.

10. R Laird Harris, Archer Jr., Gleason L, Bruce Kl. Waltke, *Theological Wordbook of the Old Testament*, 2003.

11. Bruce K. Waltke and Cathi J. Fredricks, *Genesis: A Commentary* (Grand Rapids, Mich: Zondervan, 2001).

12. Andrew E. Hill and John H. Walton, *A Survey of the Old Testament*, 3rd ed (Grand Rapids, Mich: Zondervan Publishing House, 2009), 113.

13. "Come Down, O Love Divine" hymn by Bianco da Siena, Public Domain

14. Frances J. Crosby, *Near the Cross*, 1869.

15. W. R. W. Stephens, *Saint John Chrysostom, His Life and Times* (CreateSpace Independent Publishing Platform, 2016).

16. Powlison, "Suffering and Psalm 119," 4.

17. Powlison, 5.

18. Powlison, 7.

19. C. H Spurgeon, *The Treasury of David: An Expository and Devotional Commentary on the Psalms.* (Grand Rapids, Mich.: Baker Book House, 1981), 525.

20. C. H. Spurgeon, *The Treasury of David*, vol. 1 (Nashville, Tennessee: Thomas Nelson, Inc, n.d.).

21. Tremper Longman, *Psalms: An Introduction and Commentary*, Tyndale Old Testament Commentaries, Volumes 15-16 (Downers Grove: IVP Academic/ InterVarsity Press, 2014), 313–14.

22. Spurgeon, *The Treasury of David*, 525.

23. Arthur Bennett, ed., *The Valley of Vision: A Collection of Puritan Prayers and Devotions* (Edinburgh: Banner of Truth Trust, 1975), 173. Used with permission.

24. Horatius Bonar, *A Word to Fellow Pastors and Other Christian Leaders*, n.d.

25. Charles Haddon Spurgeon, *Sermons*, vol. 10, vol. 5.

26. Tremper Longman, *How to Read the Psalms* (Downers Grove, Ill: InterVarsity Press, 1988), 73.

27. Longman, 73.

28. John Piper, "The Covenant of Abraham," *Desiring God*, October 18, 1981.

29. Piper.

30. Barbara R Duguid, Wayne Duguid Houk, and Iain M Duguid, *Prone to Wander: Prayers of Confession and Celebration*, 2014, 56–57.

31. John Murray, *Principles of Conduct: Aspects of Biblical Ethics* (Grand Rapids, Mich.: Eerdmans, 2003), 236–37.

32. Spurgeon, *The Treasury of David*, 283.

33. Spurgeon, 270.

34. Sinclair Ferguson, *Grow in Grace* (Colorado Springs, Colo.: NavPress, 1984), 36.

35. Jerry Bridges, *The Joy of Fearing God*, 1st ed (Colorado, Springs, Colo: WaterBrook Press, 1998), 19.

36. Bridges, 26.

37. Spurgeon, *The Treasury of David*, 270.

38. Bridges, *The Joy of Fearing God*, 59.

39. Bennett, *The Valley of Vision*, 196. Used with permission.

40. Paul E. Miller, *A Loving Life: In a World of Broken Relationships* (Wheaton, Illinois: Crossway, 2014), 24–27.

41. Miller, 41.

42. Augustine, "Pastor's Prayer for 16 June 2019," preachthestory.com, n.d.

43. Scotty Smith, *Everyday Prayers: 365 Days to a Gospel-Centered Faith* (Grand Rapids, MI: Baker Books, 2011), 172.

Made in the USA
Middletown, DE
22 February 2020